# *Success and the Christian*

The Cost and Criteria of
Spiritual Maturity

## A.W. Tozer

### Compiled by James L. Snyder

CHRISTIAN PUBLICATIONS
CAMP HILL, PENNSYLVANIA

Christian Publications
3825 Hartzdale Drive, Camp Hill, PA 17011

The mark of ✝ vibrant faith

ISBN: 0-87509-537-2
LOC Catalog Card Number: 93-74750
© 1994 by Christian Publications
All rights reserved
Printed in the United States of America

94 95 96 97 98  5  4  3  2  1

Cover Design: Step One Design

# CONTENTS

1  Spiritual Perfection Defined  1

2  He Is a Jealous Lover  13

3  Formula for Spiritual Success  35

4  Plague, the Terror Word  49

5  The Deeper Life  65

6  Unity That Brings Revival  85

7  Five Rules for Holy Living  101

8  Communion of Saints  117

9  The Secret of Victory  131

*The Cloud of Unknowing*

1. MAGNIFY GOD   2. MORTIFY FLESH   3. SIMPLIFY LIFE

RELATIONSHIP W/ JESUS:
1) JUDICIAL  2) VITAL  3) VOLITIONAL  4) EMOTIONAL  5.) INTELLECTUAL

UNITY OF SPIRIT ⟹ POWER

UNITY - W/ CHRIST AS THE CENTER

BE EXALTED, O GOD

p. 17, 25 A. B. Simpson — his power &
greatness lay in his unquenchable
love for the person of the Lord.

"Himself"

What I need to live (material) p. 26
GRACE + MERCY      P. 98

# SUCCESS AND
# THE CHRISTIAN

p. 76 Read the letters of Samuel
        Rutherford. (He loved
                                    God.)
p. 78 "He (Paul) loved them only
in the margin of his heart; he
loved God @ the center. He loved
them for God's dear sake. This
is Christianity."

p. 86 ✻ Unity of mind precedes
        the Holy Spirit.

Steps to Unity (p 95) 100
1. determine to glorify the Lord + not to seek honor
   for ourselves
2. united in absorption in the Lord's doings
3. be one in determination to see God's wonders
4. oneness of present expectation
5. submission to the Lord
6. resolution to put away everything that
                                        hinders

WORSHIP p. 119

tuned = unity / harmony
PIANO     music = Holy
                         spirit

p. 120 Music does not come to make
your piano get in tune; it comes
because your piano is in tune.
It is not the music that tunes your
piano; its the tuned piano that
makes your music.

UNITY 1st ⟹  H. SPIRIT
                        ‖
                   POWER

# CHAPTER 1

---

# Spiritual Perfection Defined

*We have much to say about this, but it is hard to explain because you are slow to learn. (Hebrews 5:11)*

Did you ever try talking to a person who didn't understand a word you were saying, who didn't know your language? You can stand and talk earnestly to him and he just shakes his head and maybe speaks one word that he's learned, meaning "I don't understand."

Well, that is the reason it is hard. The writer of Hebrews is saying we have many things to say; but I'm talking one language and you understand another. "Because you are slow to learn. In fact, though by this time you ought to be teachers, you need someone to teach you the elementary truths of God's word all over again. You need milk, not solid food!" (Hebrews 5:11b-12). I want to call attention to the phrase, "are become such" (KJV). They weren't such; but they had "become such as have need of milk, and not of strong meat" (5:12b, KJV). They had regressed and gone back to their childhood state after having, obviously, grown some. "Anyone who lives on milk," he explains, "being still an infant, is not acquainted with the teaching about righteousness. But solid food is for the mature, who by constant use have trained themselves to distinguish good from evil" (5:13-14).

He said that we are to leave the first principles, that is, the elementary instructions of the Christian faith. We are to leave them, but not leave them behind. We are not to leave them as one would leave one house and go to another or leave one city and go to another. We are to leave them behind as a builder who is building a house lays the foundation and leaves it behind as he goes upward. If it's a building like some of the buildings downtown, they leave the foundation far behind and go up several stories until they have thirty, forty or fifty stories towering in the air. They have left the foundation, not that they've departed from it, but they have built upon it. Now that is what the man of God means.

## The First Principles

What are these first principles that we are to leave? He names them for us so there is no misunderstanding. He says, "repentance . . . faith . . . baptisms, the laying on of hands, the resurrection of the dead, and eternal judgment" (6:1-2). These are the elementary first principles of the doctrine and we are to leave them as a builder leaves the foundation and builds on up. "Not laying again the foundation" (6:1), he says. The structure must rest on the foundation, no matter how high it may tower into the sky.

It rests upon the foundation of Christ—of who He is and of repentance and faith in Him; of baptism into the body of Christ; of the coming resurrection of the dead and the judgment to come. These are basic doctrines of the faith that we rest upon, and no matter how far we go in the Christian faith we never leave them. They are there as a foundation upon which we build.

The trouble was the Hebrews never went beyond the foundation. And this exclusive preoccupation with elementary truth is also characteristic of evangelicals today. Conversely, the ignoring of Christian truth is characteristic of the liberals. But exclusive preoccupation with the first principles is characteristic of the average church. He says that keeps us babies all our lives.

## Remaining a Baby

Let's first explore the metaphor about a baby and milk. It is possible to be frozen in your babyhood state, to have your growth suspended and stay right there. Notice the marks of a baby—beautiful in a baby, but terrible in a person when they get to be eighteen or twenty years old.

First, a baby can't concentrate on anything very long. A baby loses interest about as fast as it's possible to lose interest. It'll scream and yell and grab for something delightedly and get it, and ninety seconds later, throw it down and look for something else. That is typical of a baby and it's the way God meant a baby to be. But He didn't mean the baby's father to be like that, nor the baby's mother—nor

even the baby's seven-year-old sister. That is characteristic of a baby and it is also characteristic of
Christians who became Christians, fundamental
Christians, and then froze and stopped developing.
They're unable to stick to spiritual exercises. They
can't pray very long and can't meditate. In fact, they
smile at the whole idea of meditation. They think
that was for Thomas Aquinas. As for Bible reading,
they don't do it very much—nor very much else that
takes discipline and maturity.

    A second thing about a baby is that it is preoc-
cupied with simple things, with foundational
things. You never talk to a baby about existentialism
or the cold war. The baby is satisfied with a half a
dozen little things; it is enough to eat and to keep
warm and dry and to keep its mother within yelling
distance. That is about all a baby cares about.

    There are Christians who grow up and have no
relish for anything spiritually advanced. They're
preoccupied with their first lessons. The average
church is a school with only one grade and that is
the first one. These Christians never expect to get
beyond that and they don't want to hear a man very
long who wants to take them beyond that. If their
pastor insists they do their homework and get ready
for the next grade, they begin to pray that the Lord
will call "our dear brother" somewhere else. The
more they hate him the more they bear down on the
words "our dear brother." All he's trying to do is
prepare them for another grade, but that church is
dedicated to the first grade, and the first grade is
where it's going to remain.

Paul said some of them went up into the second grade and gave it up, and said, "It's too hard here," and they went back to the first.

"How long have you been in the first grade, Junior?"

"Twelve years."

Well, how long have you been listening to the same truth and hearing the same doctrine? You must be born again and there's a judgment and so on. While that is true and we must not leave that, we must use that to advance. But we don't do it. Whole generations of Christians grow up in the first grade. They learn to read their Bible in the light of this. To them, nothing in the Bible ever means anything beyond this elementary stage. They have Bible conferences dedicated to the first grade in the Christian life, Bible schools dedicated to the continuance of the first grade. For my part, I feel that I want a little ambition, a little spiritual ambition. Paul said, "Forgetting what is behind . . . I press on toward the goal" (Philippians 3:13b-14a). There was a man not satisfied with the first grade.

3. Another thing about a baby is its cry for amusement. It loves to be amused. When I'm on a bus somewhere I'm delighted to see a baby looking over a mother's shoulder. If the mother sees me, I just sit there dignified as can be. But if I can see the baby, I begin to do things that invariably rouse the baby and we have a good time. Finally, the mother notices him and pulls him down and wonders who that old fellow is back there. Well, I won't harm the baby; it loves to be amused. It doesn't take $100 to do it. You

can do it by wiggling your finger or looking through your fingers at it.

Just as babies love to be amused, so the cry for amusement in religion is evidence that we are frozen in the first grade. We're still children and we're going to remain that way. Children have to have toys and they have to have novelties and they have to have new playmates every once in a while. And the Church is like that.

Religious entertainment has so corrupted the Church of Christ that millions don't know that it's a heresy. Millions of evangelicals throughout the world have devoted themselves to religious entertainment. They don't know that it's as much a heresy as the counting of beads or the splashing of holy water or something else. To expose this, of course, raises a storm of angry protest among the people.

A Christian businessman once said to me, "Brother Tozer, I don't make a god out of you; but I follow you and believe you. What I'd like to know is why so many people like you but don't know what you're talking about." And I said, "Brother, I give up, I have no idea why it is." But it's true. As soon as they think you're exposing the love of religious entertainment, you're finished in a minute.

One man wrote an article as an exposé of me. He said that I claimed that religious entertainment was wrong and he said, "Don't you know that every time you sing a hymn, it's entertainment?" Every time you sing a hymn? I don't know how that fellow ever finds his way home at night. He ought to have a seeing eye dog and a man with a white cane to take him home!

When you raise your eyes to God and sing, "Break Thou the bread of life, dear Lord, to me," is that entertainment—or is it worship? Isn't there a difference between worship and entertainment? The church that can't worship must be entertained. And men who can't lead a church to worship must provide the entertainment. That is why we have the great evangelical heresy here today—the heresy of religious entertainment.

And then there is another characteristic of immaturity—a child can neither read nor enjoy advanced literature, even when they get to be five or six years old. He'll come and make you sit, he'll read the book through, but all it says is, "I saw a cat and the cat was white." You know, there's nothing much to it. It's nothing profound. If he never went beyond that, you'd feel very bad for your child. When he first comes home and says, "Mommy, Daddy, listen to me read," no matter what you are doing or what's burning on the stove, he grabs you and pulls you down and reads. He can read! How proud you are! He can read, wonderful! You never thought he'd make it, but he did; now he can read the whole book. We never knew how much our kids memorized and fooled us! But anyhow, they were reading.

Suppose ten years from now he comes in—now he's seventeen—and says, "Mommy, Daddy, I can read—'The cat is red.' "

You'd say to your husband or wife, "I think we ought to do something for this boy. I think we ought to take him somewhere."

That is exactly why the Holy Spirit wrote the book

of Hebrews. He said, "Let's leave this." Why stay where you are and remain forever engrossed in the fundamentals of religion? We excuse anything by repeating, "You've got to be born again." We can have any kind of show and say, "Now, you ought to be born again"—first principles all over. The Holy Spirit says, "Therefore, leaving the principles of the doctrine of Christ, let us go on toward perfection, not laying again these early foundations of the doctrines of Christ," and so on, "But let us go on unto perfection."

Now how shall we go on?

## Obtaining Perfection

Perfection means maturity. Just as when your son stands twenty-one years old and has his college degree, he's as healthy as they come and good-natured and well-balanced and you are proud of that big boy. What's happened to him is he's matured, that is all. But he's not perfect. Go into his room in the morning and see if what you see lying around there is perfect. He steps out of his trousers and leaves them there and his shoes over here. He's not perfect; but he's mature. He's come up to his maturity now and you're happy. You feel good and if you're a Christian, you thank God "my boy stands tall and straight and mature now and healthy."

That is what the Holy Spirit means. He doesn't mean become a wax saint without a speck of imperfection, without a freckle on your soul. He means maturing in God. Grow up in God so that you're no longer a baby, having to be entertained with the first principles. You are now growing up in God, becoming a strong Christian, learning to carry heavy burdens in the Holy Spirit, to pray effectively, to suffer with the world and with the church, and to carry the cross.

How do I go about it? Let me give several suggestions.

1. One is to make up your mind, to decide. By deciding, you can't save yourself, but you can decide to get saved and you can make up your mind after you are saved to go on with God. Until our minds are made up, God won't work with us. Or if He does, He will work toward getting it made up. Make up your mind. Get the loose ends tied up and get ready.

When a young man is called into the army, he gets that nice little letter—a beautifully worded, fraternal, nice-sounding letter—but it all means the same thing: "you're in." Before this young fellow goes he fixes up his room and has a last date with his girlfriend and goes down where he hangs out sometimes, talks to the boys and says, "Well, I'll be seeing you in two years." And he gets ready. He says his goodbyes and gets ready.

A Christian must make up his mind to go on with God and to grow up into God and learn the deep and high and lofty things of God. He must say to himself, "I've fooled around in kindergarten long enough. I've been a kindergarten Christian long enough now. I want to grow until I know what God's talking about and the high, lofty things of the Spirit."

2. The second thing is to put away unChristlike

things. Put away unChristlike habits and acts, squelch within you unChristlike desires, put away unChristlike plans and get rid of hindrances and thoughts and thought habits.

③   The third thing is to become preoccupied with the Scriptures, the Word of God. This Book of God is a powerful thing, powerful indeed. If you read it, it will bring you out and take you along. When we sing, "Break Thou the Bread of Life," we're praying that God will give us an understanding of the Scriptures. And then, pushing it on a bit and raising it to its mystical phase, we're saying, "Lord, when we take Communion, break Thou the Bread to me." That is all the same. So get preoccupied with the Scriptures. Don't just have a chapter occasionally; but read it until it warms your heart. Read it until it begins to talk to you. We haven't read the Scripture until it begins to talk to us. We only think we have. So, get preoccupied with the Scriptures. Get a good large text Bible and I recommend King James; but there are other good versions besides the King James; the King James is a good basic version always to have around and trust.

④   The fourth thing is take up your cross. Learn how to suffer for the Lord's sake a little bit. The reason the communists are slowly encroaching on us in the Western world is that we love our comforts too much. [Sermon originally preached in early 1960s.] They're not looking for comforts; they're looking for victory.

A friend of mine went to see a man who was the head of a local communist cell in a local communist headquarters where they send out literature. The communist said, "Come in, Reverend, and sit down." He went in and sat. "Now, we're communists," he said, "you know that, and you're a minister. Of course, we're miles apart. But," he said, "I want to tell you something. We learned our technique from your book of Acts." He said, "We learned how to win and conquer from your book of Acts." And he said, "You who believe the Bible have thrown overboard the methods of the early church and we who don't believe it have adopted them and they're working."

What was the method? It's a very simple method of the early church. It was to go witness, give everything to the Lord and give up all to God and bear your cross, take the consequences. The result was in the first hundred years of the Christian church the whole known world was evangelized. We don't know that now because our missionaries are telling us, or at least they're leaving the impression, that there are parts of the world that were not evangelized. Every part of the known world was evangelized about one hundred years after our Lord's resurrection.

The next thing is to get Christ in your focus, get the Lord Jesus Christ in your focus.

> Show me Thy face,
> one transient gleam of loveliness divine.
> And I will never think or dream
> of any love save Thine.

Open your heart to the Holy Spirit and I'm sure God will take you on. And remember, this isn't a luxury. This is a necessity that we forsake the first principles and give up our childhood and go on into God; it is basic necessity. For "It is impossible for those who have once been enlightened, who have tasted the heavenly gift . . . if they fall away, to be brought back to repentance" (Hebrews 6:4, 6a).

So this doctrine, this teaching, this exhortation by the Holy Spirit to leave the first principles and go on toward perfection is not to make deluxe saints. It is to make any kind of saints, a most basic necessity in the Christian life.

## CHAPTER 2

# He Is a Jealous Lover / ISHI

*But whatever was to my profit I now consider loss for the sake of Christ. What is more, I consider everything a loss compared to the surpassing greatness of knowing Christ Jesus my Lord, for whose sake I have lost all things. I consider them rubbish, that I may gain Christ and be found in him, not having a righteousness of my own that comes from the law, but that which is through faith in Christ—the righteousness that comes from God and is by faith. I want to know Christ and the power of his resurrection and the fellowship of sharing in his sufferings, becoming like him in his death, and so, somehow, to attain to the resurrection from the dead.*

*Not that I have already obtained all this, or have already been made perfect, but I press on to take hold of that for which Christ Jesus took hold of me. Brothers, I do not consider myself yet to have taken hold of it. But one thing I do: Forgetting what is behind and straining toward what is ahead, I press on toward the goal to win the prize for which God has called me heavenward in Christ Jesus.*

*All of us who are mature should take such a view
of things. And if on some point you think differently, that too God will make clear to you.
(Philippians 3:7-15)*

In discussing the issue of spiritual success, I am
allowing a six-hundred-year-old book to help us
along the way called *The Cloud of Unknowing*. I
am basing my teaching on the New Testament but I
am allowing this old brother to help us a little along
the way. I give you a motto from this ancient devotional work for your consideration: "He is a jealous
lover and He suffereth no rivals."

Paul wrote, "That I may know him" (Philippians
3:10, KJV). The word, "know" means acquaint or
acquaintance. It also means "experience." You may
be acquainted with a man and yet not have experienced the man in any sense at all. If I introduce
you, for instance, to my lifelong friend, you could
say, "Yes, I'm acquainted with him." But you have
not experienced him in the sense that I have, running around with him, traveling with him in his car,
preaching with him and going with him here and
there and talking with him numbers of times and
praying with him. There's a difference between acquaintance and experience.

To get acquainted with God is one thing; but to go
on to experience God in intensity and richness of
acquaintance is something more. Paul said, "I want
to know Him in that depth and rich intensity of
experience." As I have said many times, personality
can't be fully known with one encounter. You may

meet some people you don't particularly like at first. After you get to know them, you get to like them because you find the hidden potential in their personality that you didn't know were there. Christ is capable of increasing intimacy of acquaintance.

## Not Going On

If I have anything to say to the Church of Christ in general it is this: that our great weakness is that not only are we not going on to know Christ in rich intimacy of acquaintance but we're not even talking about it. We don't even hear about it. It doesn't get into our magazines. It doesn't get into our books. It doesn't get onto our radios. It's not found in our churches—this yearning, this longing to know Him in increasing measure. Now we may enjoy this increasing acquaintance with the "that."

You may say, "But Jesus Christ is a He, a Person. Why do you call Him 'That'? " You may not understand me now, but Paul says, "if . . . you think differently, *that* too God will make clear to you" (3:15, italics added). Before we can know God as a "He" we must know Him as "That." I think every theologian would agree with me here. I find in the book of Luke these words addressed to the virgin Mary: "That holy thing which shall be born of thee" (1:35b, KJV). And John, not an amateur theologian but the man who had laid his head upon the breast of Jesus, begins his wondrous first epistle with the word "That." "That which was from the beginning, which we have heard, which we have seen with our eyes, which we have looked at and our hands have touched . . . the Word of life" (1 John 1:1). Personality is not found there yet. "The life appeared; we have seen it and testify to it, and we proclaim to you the eternal life, which was with the Father and has appeared to us. We proclaim to you what we have seen and heard, so that you also may have fellowship with us. And our fellowship is with the Father and with his Son, Jesus Christ" (1:2-3). It's not until the last two lines of the third verse that he puts personality in there. It's "That" before.

Remember, my friends, Jesus Christ, while He is a Person, and is the eternal Son of God, He is also "That" which is the source of everything. He is "That" which is the foundation and fountain of everything you and I are created to enjoy. He is the Fountain of all truth; but He is more—He is Truth itself. He is the Source and Spring of all beauty; but He is more—He is Beauty itself. He is the Fountain of all wisdom; but He is more—He is Wisdom itself and in Him are all the treasures of wisdom and knowledge hidden away. He is the Fountain of all grace. He is the Fountain and Source of all life. But He is more than that. He said, "I am the bread of life" (John 6:35) and "I am . . . the life" (11:25). He is the Fountain of love; but He is more than that—He is Love. He is the Resurrection. He is Immortality and He is, as the song says, "Brightness of my Father's glory, sunshine of my Father's face."

We try to discover what gets wrong with us when we start to backslide in groups, denominations, churches and individuals. I believe that our Lord Jesus hit it on the head when He said, "You have

forsaken your first [degree of] love" (Revelation 2:4).
Not your first love consecutively in the sense that
there's love #1 and love #2 and love #3; but He said,
"You have forsaken your first *degree of* love."

What I'm preaching to try to bring about in the
Church of Jesus Christ is a rediscovery of the loveli-
ness of the Savior that we might begin to love Him
again with the intensity of love such as our fathers
knew. I have said before and I repeat it now that the
power and greatness of A.B. Simpson was not in his
theology for he positively was not a great theologian
compared, for instance, with John Calvin or some of
the other theologians. The power and greatness of
the man lay in his unquenchable love for the Person
of Jesus Christ the Lord.

There's a song we sing and I want to read two
stanzas that we know about. The first stanza says:

> Fairest Lord Jesus,
> Ruler of all nature,
> O Thou of God and man the Son.
> Thee will I cherish,
> Thee will I honor,
> Thou my soul's glory, joy, and crown.

We know that one and two others but there are
others that we don't know and here's one:

> Fair are the flowers,
> Fair are Earth's children,
> When viewed in this sun-clouded day.
> Yet they must perish,

All will soon vanish,
Jesus alone abides for aye.

Gaze out upon the world, on your family, your
friends, your loved ones, all the lovely beauty of
children and young people viewed in earth's sun-
clouded day. Yet candor and realism compel us to
say, "Yet they must perish, All will soon vanish."
And when they have vanished, we have only Jesus
who "alone abides for aye."

Earth's fairest beauty,
Heaven's brightest splendor
Who Jesus Christ unfolded see,
All that here shineth
Quickly declineth
Before His spotless purity.

There are those who would trouble you because
you can't get all steamed up about material things.
A friend of mine was quite irked because I just can't
get all excited and steamed up about earthly things.
I can't possibly do it. I can't possibly stand off and
strike an attitude of awe at a Buick or a Cadillac or
something else. I can't. The houses they're building
that are supposed to be so magnificent, I can't get
excited about them. When you have seen the house
or city that has foundations whose builder and
maker is God (Hebrews 11:10), you can't get excited
about any house any man in this world ever built.
You can't get excited about it. Abraham saw the city
that had foundations whose builder and maker was

God and he wouldn't build a house after that. He said "I will never try to imitate. I will live in a tent until I get my house up there." It was so beautiful. Well, "Earth's fairest beauty and Heaven's brightest splendor" are all unfolded in Jesus Christ. And "all that here shineth quickly declineth before His spotless purity." That's what one man said about Jesus.

## It Costs to Know Jesus

I want to tell you that it costs to know Jesus Christ like that. It costs, and most people won't pay the price for it at all. That's why most Christians are common. They won't go on because for Christ's sake, they have surrendered evil things—that is, things that are injurious and things that are unclean and grossly sinful; but they are unwilling to surrender "good things." Everywhere in fundamentalism we have given up the grossly sinful things. We have all agreed on what those grossly sinful things are. We shudder at the thought of a honkytonk, though there are some churches and tabernacles that you couldn't tell the difference if somebody didn't yell "Jesus" occasionally to give it a holy atmosphere. Honky-tonks and unholy places, we stay out of them.

There are certain things we don't do and for Christ's sake we have surrendered those evil things. But this is the mark of a common Christian and the man who's never gone beyond that is a mediocre Christian. Paul surrendered the good along with the bad. He said, "Not only the things that are bad have I given up; but what things were gain to me those I counted loss." The things that he had a right to, the things that were gain to him and that he had every legal and moral right to lay hold of and say, "This is mine and Christianity is not going to take it from me." Paul said, "I've given up even that because I've seen something so much better. It is that which was with the Father. It is that Source, that Fountain from which flows all wisdom and beauty and truth and immortality. So for the sake of 'That,' I have given it all up." Paul knew the human heart was idolatrous and would worship anything it possessed. Anything that you get your hand on you will worship.

As a little child will take his teddy bear to bed with him, so we grownups have our "teddy bears" too. We were too grown up and mature, you know, to be caught taking a teddy bear or doll to bed. We have what to God must look like teddy bears and dolls. We hang onto them. A baby, of course, has a right to that. I believe in that. We kept teddy bears floating around for years at our home until our children outgrew them, and they were pretty old when they did. But the point I'm making is that we oldsters, we mature people, people even in their teens, when we still insist upon hanging on to things we will worship them. Whatever you hang on to, you worship because it gets between you and God, whether it be property or family or reputation or security or your life itself. Jesus taught that we couldn't even hang on to our life itself. If we made our living on earth to be something that we wouldn't give up and hung on to, it would get in our way and we'd lose ourselves in that.

Then there's grasping after security. We want to be

secure. Paul wasn't secure. He said he died daily. He was driven by the sea for three weeks, night and day, and was always in difficulty. But we have this longing for security, security in this life and eternal security in the world above. Brethren, Paul said, "I give it all up. I disavow and disown everything."

## *Treasures That Touch Your Heart*

There are certain things God let Paul have. He let him have a book or two, let him have a coat, and let him have his own hired house for two years in one instance. He let him have some things; but Paul never allowed those things to touch his heart. Any external treasure that touches your heart is a curse. Paul said, "I give that up so that I might know Him. That I might go on to deeply enriched and increasing intimacy and vast expanses of knowledge of the One who is intimate and illimitable in His beauty and I go on to know Him. And that I might know Him, I give all this up." He never allowed anything to touch his heart.

We have been taught over the last years, in our Christian circles, that Christ is something added on to a happy, jolly, rather clean but worldly earthly life to save us from hell and to get us into the mansions over there. That's not the New Testament way of looking at things. It's not the way Paul looked at it at all. Paul considered Jesus Christ to be so infinitely attractive that he didn't count anything at all to amount to anything. Paul was a learned man. He learned at the feet of Gamaliel. He had what they'd call now a Ph.D. Paul said, "That's all dross." He used an ugly word—"garbage." He said, "It's no good; I put it all behind me." And he said, "I'm of the Tribe of Benjamin and circumcised the eighth day and I belong to the fathers. I've got the marks upon me and my name's in the register and I can show you who I am. But for the sake of Jesus Christ, I count that nothing at all. I put that under my feet."

Some of you are proud of your Dutch blood and that's why you're carnal all the time. Some of you are proud of your Swedish blood and that's why you're carnal all the time. And some of you are proud of some other blood. All blood's the same kind: corrupt. I don't care whether it comes from royalty or from the gutter; it's corrupt blood. We are proud of things and proud of what we can do. Paul said, "Everything—the proudest thing I have, the thing of which I am the proudest, I count it but loss."

Modern Christianity says, "Stop gambling or the bomb will get you. Stop drinking or you will go down like Rome. Stop this or that." You can pick out those ugly bestial things that nobody wants to do if they're in their right mind. And that's all the things there are. Paul said, "I've quit those long ago." He never even did them. He was a Jew in all good conscience and he didn't have to quit them. That's why I sometimes smile kind of sourly when I hear the testimony about somebody that drank and then he got saved and quit it. Oh, sure, it's good that he quit drinking, but that ought to be elementary. Then he writes a book on how bad he was! You can have the book. I already have all the books I want to read.

Let this old writer of *The Cloud of Unknowing* talk

to us a little bit. He says, "But the one thing I tell thee, He is a jealous lover and He suffers no rivals." Now brethren, that's what's the matter with us. We're allowing rivals to come up. No decent fellow, nobody that has any self-respect is going to suffer a rival. But he says, "God won't suffer a rival." And he says, in old English, "And Him list not work in thy will but He only would thee by Himself." Let me translate that into bad modern English: he says that God won't work in your will unless He can only be there by Himself.

## Too Many Gods

We have too many gods. We have too many irons in the fire. And we have too much theology that we don't understand. We have too much religion and too much "churchianity" and too much institutionalism and too much, too much. The result is, God isn't in there by Himself. He says, "If I'm not in your heart by Myself, I won't work." When Jesus Christ has everything cleansed from the temple and dwells there alone, He will work.

Francois Fénelon, the French mystic, wrote about God's working like a miner in the depths of the earth. Have you ever been in the coal mines? Deep down in the earth they're mining out coal or gold or diamonds and anybody can fly overhead or walk overhead or travel by and never dream of what's going on in the depths—never know there's an intelligent force at work bringing out jewels. Fénelon said that's what God does in the human breast. He works hidden and unseen within the breast.

But we're dramatic in our day. We don't want God to work unless He comes with a beard on and a staff, playing a part. We want Him to be theatrical and do the thing with a good deal of color and fireworks. God won't work like that. God says, "You children of Adam, you children of carnality and lust, you who love a fairy show in the flesh, you who have been brought up wrong and have wrong ideas about my Son, I won't work in you." Jesus said, "I can't do it. I'm sorry; I can't work in you and dwell in your heart unless I can be there alone."

What some of you need to do is cleanse the temple. You just need to get busy and clear it out—drive out the cattle and upset the money changers and shovel out the dirt and get rid of a lot of things that are rivaling the Lord Jesus Christ. Here's my motto: "He's a jealous lover and He suffereth no rivals."

The author of *The Cloud of Unknowing* goes on to say, "Lift up thine heart now unto God with a stirring of love and none of these goest and, therefore look thee lope." I looked that word "lope" up in the unabridged dictionary and it's an old Anglo-Saxon word meaning "unwilling; to be unwilling; to hate." And the meaning here is "to be unwilling to think on anything but God Himself." So nothing works in your wit nor your will that's in your head nor in your heart, but only Himself.

## Nothing but Christ

A.B. Simpson talked about "Himself" and he shocked and blessed a generation because of it. He said, "Jesus Himself. It's Himself that we need." It is interesting how the sermon and hymn "Himself" came to be written. Dr. Simpson went to London, England to a Bible conference. There were three sermons on sanctification and he preached the last one. That's a bad spot to be in. The first preacher got up and said the way to be holy and victorious in your heart was to suppress the old man, he taught suppression. The next preacher got up and taught eradication. He said deliverance from the old carnal life is by eradication and getting rid of the old man— to pull him up and turn his roots up to the sun to die. Dr. Simpson had to get in between there. So he got up and took one word for his text, "Himself." He gave his testimony about how he had tried to get the victory. He said, "Sometimes I would get it and think I had it and then I'd lose it." Then he said, "When I came to the knowledge that victory, sanctification, deliverance, purity, holiness, all is Himself, it was easy and the glory came to my life." I thought that was a beautiful piece of diplomacy and a wise way to handle a thing and good theology. Around that, he wrote his famous hymn:

> Once it was the blessing,
>   Now it is the Lord;
> Once it was the feeling,
>   Now it is His Word;
> Once His gift I wanted,
>   Now the Giver own;
> Once I sought for healing,
>   Now Himself alone.

There must be more of Himself these days. Christianity has gotten to be a way of getting things from God. For example, we give a tithe in order that our nine-tenths will go further than our ten-tenths. Ordinary business would lead you to do that, wouldn't it? That's not spirituality, that's just business. And if a man wants to be a businessman and use God why, OK. But that's not what the Bible teaches and that's not what Paul talked about. Paul had given up that years before. That's not what the old writer of *The Cloud of Unknowing* talked about. He said, "It's only Himself."

I'm not condemning my good friends of the Christian Businessmen's Committee nor my good and loved friends who edit their magazine, but I say they are in danger. Christian businessmen can get to thinking of Christianity as a way to have a prosperous business down here and a mansion in the sky—either way you win. They can get to thinking that if you follow the Lord, you will prosper down here.

To follow the Lord doesn't always mean that. In fact, I would say it rarely means to have financial prosperity. But following the Lord has meant down the years to "consider everything a loss compared to the surpassing greatness of knowing Christ Jesus" (Philippians 3:8). And where a fellow prospers in spite of himself, then the way he gets around it is to give everything away, as much as he can at least. He keeps enough to live on, thanks God he's still here, body and soul held together and a place to live and a car to take him to church and to work; but further than that, he's not much concerned.

We have made Christianity to be a way, a technique by which we can get things. Paul didn't—he knew better than that. He said, "What is more, I consider everything a loss compared to the surpassing greatness of knowing Christ Jesus my Lord, for whose sake I have lost all things. I consider them rubbish, that I may gain Christ and . . . know Christ and the power of his resurrection" (3:8, 10a). It's all Himself. As for anything else in this life, the author of *The Cloud of Unknowing* says, "Let them be and take no heed to them."

That's why you can't get anywhere in your Christian life. That's why some of you who read this are going to put this book down, because we're getting too close to where you live. You'd like to have a deeper life that could be given to you with a syringe or a glass of water and a pill. "Take one pill three times a day." You just can't do that. But that is the way some people get their religion. They want it in pill form, so they buy books. Brethren, there is no such thing. There's a cross, there's a gallows, there's a man with stripes on His back, there's an apostle with no property. There's a tradition of loneliness and weariness and rejection and glory. But there are no pills. It is only Himself, Himself, Himself.

I'd like to see somewhere or recapture once more before I die, the glory that men knew of the beauty of Jesus. One old brother said this about it:

Many beauteous names thou bearest,
Brother, Shepherd, Friend and King,

but then none unto my spirit
such divine support can bring.

Ishi, Ishi, is the jewel,
Mine He is while ages roll.
Angels taste not of such glory,
Holy Ishi of the soul.

Other joys are short and fleeting
Thou and I can never part.
Thou art altogether lovely,
Ishi, Ishi of my heart. (see Hosea 2:16, KJV)

They sang that once. Where could you sing that now? I think we could sing it here, but there aren't many places where you can sing it because people don't have the experience that it conveys and embodies. Whenever a good song is rejected, it's rejected because the people don't understand it and they find it dull. If you like rock 'n roll, you won't like "Ishi." And if you like, "Tenderly He watches over me," you won't like "Ishi." And if you like "He," you won't like "Ishi." "Ishi is the jewel. Mine He is while ages roll. Angels taste not of such glory, Holy Ishi of the soul."

## The Deeper Life

This is the teaching of the deeper life—to "put away all the creatures that ever God made" and stop trying to promote your family. Stop trying to promote your business and use God to do it. Stop trying to promote anything and use God to do it; put everything away but God. "For He list not work in thy heart unless He can be there alone." Put everything else out.

Some young preacher will study until he has to get thick glasses to take care of his failing eyesight because he has an idea he wants to become a famous preacher. He wants to use Jesus Christ to make him a famous preacher. He's just a huckster buying and selling and getting gain. They will ordain him and he will be known as Reverend and if he writes a book, they will make him a doctor. And he will be known as Doctor; but he's still a huckster buying and selling and getting gain. And when the Lord comes back, He will drive him out of the temple along with the other cattle.

We can use the Lord for anything—or try to use Him. But what I'm preaching and what Paul taught and what was brought down through the years and what gave breath to the modern missionary movement that you and I know about and belong to was just the opposite: "O, God, we don't want anything You have, we want You." That's the cry of a soul on its way up.

In England there is a bird called the skylark. The skylark will fly higher and higher and sing as it ascends and the poets have said that the skylark ascends and sings hymns at heaven's gate. It ascends until it's out of sight and you can still hear the song coming down though you no longer see the bird. It ascends, singing as it rises. My friends, this is what I'm preaching about. But this is what most people don't want.

Another thing a man said about God was this that
I've always loved to quote:

> Love sits on His eyelids and scatters
>     delight
> Through all the wide regions above.
> Their faces the Cherubim veil in His sight
> And tremble with raptures of love.

These people who have to have truckloads of
gadgets to get their religion going, what will they do
when they don't have anything like that? The truck
can't get where they're going.

I heard a man boast this afternoon on the radio to
come to his place because they were going to bring
in equipment from Pennsylvania and Ohio to serve
the Lord with. What equipment do you need to
serve the Lord with, brother? Why, the dear old
camp meeting ladies used to say, "See, this is my
harp with ten strings and I praise the Lord!" And
they'd clap their little old wrinkled hands with shining faces. What claptrap do you need? Do you need
a bushel basket full of stuff to serve the Lord with?

Brother, if you have two knees and even if you're
stiffened up with arthritis so you can't get on your
knees, you can look up in your heart. For prayer isn't
getting on your knees—prayer is the elevation of the
heart to God. That's all a man needs. You can pray
in a prison, you can pray in an airplane, you can pray
in a ship; you can pray anywhere and you can
worship God, because it's Himself that we want,
Himself.

> Love sits on His eyelids and scatters
>     delight
> Through all the wide regions above.
> Their faces the Cherubim veil in His sight
> And tremble with raptures of love.

The only kind of revival I'm even remotely interested in is the kind of revival that will cause people to tremble with rapture in the presence of the Lord Jesus Christ.

I've been reading Proverbs devotionally every day and I've gotten into the thirteenth chapter. And I rather smiled when I read the fourth verse—"The sluggard craves and gets nothing." In the Septuagint version, the old Greek version translated into English, it reads, "Every sluggard is employed in wishing." The Knox translation says, "Idleness will and will not both at once."

Now there we have a lot of Christians. We're sluggards. And being a lifelong student, I didn't take that word "sluggard" at its face value. I looked it up to find out what a sluggard was. Well, a slug is a sort of a streamlined snail. When they crawl along, they do about a mile a millennium. They just crawl along leaving a wet streak behind them. That's a slug. Some fellow must have been looking at a lazy slug, and then when his son wouldn't work he said, "You're like that slug. You're a sluggard." And that's how we got that word in English.

And the Bible says "That every sluggard is employed in wishing." He goes to church, chases from one side of the city to the other to hear a new evangelist just hoping that he can become a spiritual man, but he's too lazy; he's a sluggard. "He will and he will not both at the same time," as Knox says. That's the way a lot of Christians are. And what can you do with them? Can you wake them up? I can't. I've tried everything I could find and I just can't wake people up. Sluggards will be sluggards till the Lord comes, I suppose.

But I think some of you are going to get some wings and get rid of the shell. I'll tell you this—if some women kept house like they keep their soul, they'd be in for a divorce. Their husbands wouldn't stay around. If some people kept their business the way they keep their souls, they'd go bankrupt.

## Your Response

What's your response? The old brother in *The Cloud of Unknowing* says this and I've found it true: If you're going to go on now, and know God and get up and stir yourself, and lift your heart to God and put away things and desire for property and things and seek Himself alone, and let Him work in you without any rivals, "all the fiends [of hell] will be furious when thou doest this. And they will try to defeat thee in all that they can do." You won't get up to the corner but what some fiend will be after you. So if you want security, don't seek God. If you want security, the devil will give it to you for a while and then send you to hell. If you're afraid of fiends and all the rest, don't try to seek God.

But he goes on to say, "Let not, therefore, but travail therein till thou see and list." By this he means, "Don't be hindered—don't let anybody hinder you in your seeking after God. Keep going until you feel desire."

It is claimed that these old saints were dreamers. They weren't dreamers; they were practical men. The author of *The Cloud of Unknowing* is saying, "When you first start to seek a new height and become something other than a common Christian, the first thing you will find [is] the devil facing you to stop you." And he adds, "Don't stop because of that, but press right on whether you feel like it or not."

There are two times to pray: when you feel like it and when you don't. Some people want to be emotionally lifted and wafted into the sky, but the old saints knew better than that. They knew that there are times when you only get through by what *The Cloud of Unknowing* calls a "naked intent unto God." That's what we need—a naked intent to know God, to know Christ, to put the world beneath our feet, to put things beneath our feet, to put people beneath our feet. To open our hearts to only one lover—the Son of God Himself—and to keep everything else out of it. All our relationships—husband and wife, father and son, mother and daughter, businessman and partner, taxpayer and citizen—all those we keep outside of ourselves. For in the deep of our hearts we have only one lover. "He suffereth no rivals."

# CHAPTER 3

---

# Formula for Spiritual Success

(1) May those who love your salvation always
    say,
    "The LORD be exalted [magnified, KJV]!"
    (Psalms 40:16b)

*MAGNIFY GOD*

(2) Put to death [mortify, KJV], therefore, whatever
belongs to your earthly nature: sexual immorality,
impurity, lust, evil desires and greed, which is
idolatry. . . .
   Slaves, obey your earthly masters in everything;
and do it, not only when their eye is on you and
to win their favor, but with sincerity of heart and
reverence for the Lord. (Colossians 3:5, 22)

*MORTIFY THE FLESH*

(3) But one thing I do: Forgetting what is behind and
straining toward what is ahead. (Philippians
3:13b)

*SIMPLIFY YOUR LIFE*

I believe that life is a serious thing, and that this
is a serious world in which we live. I am en-
couraged to believe that there are serious-
minded people still alive in the world who realize

35

the seriousness of life and are honestly concerned about how they can meet and conquer life and death and how they can salvage something out of the rest of the world and how they can save their own souls out of the disaster.

So I think there are some who are wanting to save their souls out of this untoward generation, this coming disaster in the crash and downfall of the world. Such as that would welcome counsel, and I want to give it to you. Counsel, not from a perfect man, but from somebody who's walked with God, who has loved and lived in the Scriptures for quite a while, who has no other motive except to do you good.

If you're going to save yourself from this untoward generation and salvage something out of the world wreck and the crash and fall of the world, you are going to have to do three things: the first is, magnify God; the second, mortify the flesh; and the third, simplify your life. That is what the three Scripture passages above say.

## Magnify God

Let's look at the first one first. "May those who love your salvation always say, 'The LORD be exalted [magnified, KJV]!' " (Psalms 40:16b).

I am positively sure after many years of observation and prayer that the basis of all of our trouble today, in religious circles, is that our God is too small.

When he says magnify the Lord, he doesn't mean that you are to make God big, but you are to see Him big. When we take a telescope and look at a star, we don't make the star bigger, we only see it big. Likewise you cannot make God bigger, but you are only to see Him bigger.

It is quite popular for us to say that liberals and modernists have a little God, and we evangelicals have a big God. We do have a big God, but most of us do not see Him big.

My first point is, see God big; magnify God. What is the most important verse in the Bible? It is not the one you think it is: "Jesus Christ is the same yesterday and today and forever" (Hebrews 13:8). Nor is it the other one you think it is: John 3:16, "For God so loved the world . . ." The most important verse in the Bible is this one: "In the beginning, God . . ." (Genesis 1:1). That is the most important verse, because that is where everything must begin. God is the mountain out of which everything springs, and He is the foundation upon which everything rests. God is all in all.

An old archbishop once said, "God is over all things, under all things, outside all things; within, but not enclosed, without, but not excluded; above, but not raised up, below, but not depressed; wholly above presiding, wholly beneath sustaining; wholly without embracing, and wholly within filling."

I am sure that if we all saw God bigger, we would see people smaller. This is the day of the magnification of slick personalities, and as we magnify men, we minimize God. Do not think that we have escaped the curse in evangelical circles or even in full gospel circles, for we have not. We have whole

meetings go by in which we never see God at all—
we only see His servants. And the curlier the hair of
the servant, the more we see the servant. And if he's
been pardoned from murdering his grandmother's
aunt, we magnify him still more. And if he's been
half-converted from movie acting, we magnify him
still more.

We always have some big wheel that we are down
in front of, kissing the toe of. Then we wonder why
the Holy Spirit doesn't bless us. The Holy Spirit
doesn't bless us for the same reason He doesn't bless
the Catholic for kissing the toe of the Virgin. They
have their focus wrong. We respect the Virgin, but
we do not worship her. And God would have us
respect each other, but not worship each other. There
is an awful lot of hero worship in the church of
Christ.

"Magnify the Lord with me, and everybody say,
the Lord be magnified." God moves according to
an eternal purpose; and He carries on after His own
plan. A long time ago, when the Presbyterians were
meeting somewhere in London to work up what
later was called "The Thirty-nine Articles," they
had a definition for every major point of doctrine
except one: the doctrine of God. No one could seem
to come up with a definition, and I think I can guess
why.

They were just about to despair when one
moderator pointed to a young minister down in
front and said, "Brother, would you lead us in
prayer one more time, that God might give us light
on what we can put down in the Creed about God?"

The young fellow got up and grabbed the seat ahead of him and squeezed his eyes shut and shook his head and prayed with great earnestness and said, "Oh, God, Thou art the Spirit; infinite, eternal, unchangeable in Thy being, wisdom, power, holiness, justice, goodness and truth."

Somebody said, "That is enough, that is it." And they wrote it down. So here we have it: God is the Spirit; infinite, eternal, unchangeable in His being, wisdom, power, holiness, justice, goodness and truth.

Old Novatian said, "That in the contemplation of God's majesty, all eloquence is done," which is to say that God is always greater than anything that can be said about Him. No language is worthy of Him. He is more sublime than all sublimity, loftier than all loftiness, more profound than all profundity, more splendid than all splendor, more powerful than all power, more truthful than all truth. Greater than all majesty, more merciful than all mercy, more just than all justice, more pitiful than all pity. Nothing anybody can say about Him is enough.

In Isaiah there occurs the passage, "Lift your eyes and look to the heavens: Who created all these? He who brings out the starry host one by one, and calls them each by name. Because of his great power and mighty strength, not one of them is missing" (40:26). Until someone pointed it out to me, I didn't see what was there. Isaiah uses a figure of speech that was probably the loftiest ever conceived by the mind of man. I do not think Shakespeare or David or Isaiah ever had a loftier thought than this one.

This man Isaiah saw the stars in the heavens above, as sheep on a green pasture field, and the great God Almighty, the Shepherd, walking among them and calling them all by name. And if you are not afraid that your head will split open with the effort, try to conceive the infinite number of stars that dot the heavens above. Then think of God leading the stars, as a shepherd leads his flock, calling every one by name. And not one of them is missing. This is our God.

My brethren, God calls us to magnify Him, to see Him big. A meeting is not big because a lot of people are present. A meeting is big because a number of people see a big God in the meeting. And the bigger God is seen, the greater the meeting. A friend of mine has a little saying, "I would rather have a big, little meeting than a little, big meeting." There are a lot of big meetings that are little because the God in them is a small God. And there are a lot of little meetings that are big because God is big in the midst of them.

If you are a Christian, and you are getting older in God, you ought to be getting nearer to God and God ought to be becoming to you more and more, and other things less and less. If you still have to be chucked under the chin so many times a month by the pastor to keep you happy, then you need help from God, my friend.

If God is not the biggest thing in the world to you, not all your talk will ever impress me. We ought to be where God is everything, where we walk into a meeting and see God and think God and feel God. We ought to see God all around us, where He comes down over us and we see Him in a vision, in the cool of the day. We ought to see Him in a mountain, in thunder and fire. We ought to see Him on the cross in blood and tears, and coming down through the sky, riding a white horse, and sitting on a throne judging the nations. But always, we see God and God is everything.

I want to leave behind me a flavor of God, so that God gets all the credit. When I say God I mean the triune God. Someone once accused me of talking about God all the time, while others talk about Jesus all the time. Well, I didn't answer him. I never answer a critic; I am afraid to. I know how sharp my tongue is, so I keep my mouth shut. But I know this: when I say God, I mean Jesus and the Father and the Holy Spirit. So when I talk about God, I do not split up the Godhead. You cannot divide the Godhead, brother. The old Creed said that "We are not to confound the persons nor divide the substance." And God cannot be anywhere partly present.

Wherever God is, God is all there, because you cannot divide the substance that is God. So that where the Father is, there also is the Son and the Holy Spirit. And where the Son is, there is the Father and the Holy Spirit. And where the Holy Spirit is, there is the Father and the Son. So the blessed Trinity is here—He is all here, not partly but all here. God doesn't send representatives; God Himself is here. And if that is not good news to you, you need to be born again.

That is the first thing—magnify God. Your ministry will be little, and you will live and die little unless you have a bigger God. I pray that our great God will make Himself big in our eyes, so that when we meet, our conversation will not be "shop talk"; it will be all about God.

## II. *Mortify the Flesh*

The second thing is, mortify—put to death—the flesh. Christians might as well admit that there is a reality you have got to reckon with, and that is your flesh. By flesh, *I do not mean your body*. That old monastic idea that God is angry with your body is just as silly as it can possibly be. Your body is just the goat you ride around on, that is all. It is neither good nor bad; it is just your bones and flesh and blood, that is all. It is what the thinkers and the philosophers call amoral—not moral or immoral, just neutral.

So when the Bible says, "mortify your flesh," it does not mean kill your blood and your bones and your epidermis and your hair and teeth and eyes and stomach. God is not mad at our physical body. When the Bible says, "Mortify your flesh", it means your ego, your old man, that self, that evil that is in you. That birthday present you got from the devil when you were born. That inward thing. That is your flesh.

If the old man was something that could be lifted out, like an onion could be pulled out of a garden, then we'd all feel very proud of the fact that we'd been de-onionized and debunked. But the terrible part about crucifying the flesh is, the flesh is *you*. When the Lord says mortify the flesh, He doesn't mean abuse your body by starving it or lying on beds of nails. He means, put yourself on the cross. That is what people do not want to do.

Some denominations started out believing in the doctrine of self-crucifixion, of putting ourselves to death, of mortifying the flesh through the cross of Jesus. That is all old stuff now; it belongs back there with the horse and buggy and high-button shoes. Nobody believes it anymore, or if they do, they do not live it. I think it is better not to believe it and say so, like some of our good Calvinist friends do, than to say you believe it and then live in spite of it, in defiance of it.

There are a lot of people trying to get away with the old man. What do I mean by the old man? I mean your pride, your bossiness, your nastiness, your temper, your mean disposition, your lustfulness and your quarrelsomeness. What do I mean, Reverend? I mean your study, your hunting for a bigger church, being dissatisfied with the offering and blaming the superintendent because you cannot get called. The reason you cannot get called is nobody wants you. That is what I mean, Reverend.

Deacons, what do I mean? I mean sitting around in board meetings wearing your poor pastor out, because you are too stubborn to humble yourself and admit you are wrong.

What do I mean, musicians? I mean that demeanor that makes you hate somebody that can sing a little better than you can. I mean that jealousy that makes you want to play the violin when everybody knows you can't, especially the choir director. You hate him, wish he were dead, and secretly pray that he would get called to Punxsutawney. That is what I mean. All of this may be under the guise of spirituality and we may have learned to put our head over on one side, fold our hands gently and put on a beatific smile like St. Francis of Assisi, and still be just as carnal as they come.

I do not know why you fear sanctification and I do not care. But I do say this: you had better mortify your flesh, or your flesh will do something terrible to you. In these terrible days in which we live, we have not only accepted the flesh in its morally fine manifestation as being quite proper, but we have created an ignoble theology of "extenuating circumstances," by which we excuse the flesh.

People do not hesitate any more to say, "Oh, was I mad!" and then a minute later, lead in prayer. But he is just mumbling words. I have no confidence in a man who loses his temper. I do not believe that a man who blows up and loses his temper is a spiritual man, whether he is a preacher, a bishop or a pope. He is a carnal man and needs to be cleansed by fire and blood. But we have excused people who say, "I was mad." If you were mad, you were sinning and you need to be cleansed from your bad temper. But we have incorporated the flesh into our orthodoxy, and instead of being humble, we magnify the proud fellow.

Years ago God gave me an ice pick and said, "Now Son, among your other duties will be to puncture all the inflated egos you see. Go stick an ice pick in them." And there has been more popping and hissing in my ministry as the air goes out of egos. People hate me for that, but I love them for the privilege of whittling them down to size, because if there is anything that we ought to get straight, it is how little we are.

When I was a young fellow, I always loved guns. I had a .22 revolver and loved to shoot. Just for fun when I had nothing else to do, and that is rare now, I would go out shooting with another fellow, and we shot what we called a mud hen. It looked like a great big duck, but when we dressed it, it was the biggest hypocrite you ever saw. It was practically all feathers. It was not much bigger than an oversized robin when we got down to the real bird. That describes most Christians. We stand our feathers on end so people do not know how small we are.

The word mortify comes from the same Latin word as mortuary—a place where you put dead people. It means to die. But we do not talk about that much any more. We talk about it, but we do not believe in getting reduced. But you will never be a spiritual man until God reduces you to your proper size.

Mortify is a New Testament word. Turn your back upon yourself and reckon yourself to be dead indeed and crucified with Christ. Then expect the blood of Christ and the power of the Holy Spirit to make real what your faith has reckoned. And then begin to live it. Some people go to an altar and get sanctified, but they're still resentful, they still have a chip on their shoulder. They still love money. They still have a temper. They still look where they should not. And then they claim to be sanctified. They are just pretenders, or worse than that, they are deceived persons. Either we mortify the flesh, or the flesh will harm us to a point where we have no power, no joy, no fruit, no usefulness, no victory.

## Simplify Your Life

Start by simplifying your life. Practically everyone has too much, knows too much, sees too much, hears too much, goes to too many places and comes back from too many places. We must simplify our lives or we are going to lose terribly.

Life has a center and a perimeter. At the center of the soul you will find God. Then there is an outer court and the fields and the woods and the deserts beyond. Most people do not live in the center of their lives. "Be still and know that I am God" (Psalm 46:10a), is the great Bible word. Most people would be afraid of backsliding if they would quit yelling. If they got still, just long enough to listen to the voice of God, they would feel that theirs was the coldest meeting in all the world.

Some of the most wonderful meetings in the world are where God is there in such awful power people are afraid to speak. Some of the most wonderful meetings I've ever been in have been meetings where nobody would even whisper. The mighty power of God was there and nobody dared open his mouth. When I am praying the most eloquently, I am getting the least accomplished in my prayer life. But when I stop getting eloquent and give God less theology and shut up and just gaze upward and wait for God to speak to my heart He speaks with such power that I have to grab a pencil and a notebook and take notes on what God is saying to my heart.

The further we get out from the center of our lives, the more speed we get and the less power. Anyone who knows machinery knows that if you have a little wheel on a power shaft you have less speed, but you have more power. If you have a big wheel on the power shaft, you have more speed, but you have less power. That is why you shift gears in your car—you have more power when you are in a low gear, but you have more speed when you are in a higher gear, because you are out further from the center. And so it is with God's people.

The further you get out from the center of your heart, and from the presence of God, and from the sanctuary of your soul, the faster you go, but the less power you have. Most people like to go fast, they do not care for power. Socrates was in Athens and somebody took him around Athens' 10-cent stores. After half a day of paddling around in his old bare feet, they let him sit down and rest. Then they said, "Socrates, what do you think of it?"

He replied, "I never knew before how many things there are in Athens that I do not want." Now I like that, don't you? But many today are too busy, know too much and read too many things.

Some say I am a radical, but I've been called radical since I was nineteen. Let me give you some advice. Do you know how you can have a stepped-up revival in your soul? Go home and pull the plug out on your radio and TV and leave it out for ten full days. I do not say to throw out these things. I almost said to go home and pull the plug out of the telephone, but I will not say that—though maybe that is necessary. But at least go home and pull the plug out on your TV and radio. Then get alone with God and discover Him for the first time.

# CHAPTER 4

# Plague, the Terror Word

*When famine or plague comes to the land, or blight or mildew, locusts or grasshoppers, or when an enemy besieges them in any of their cities, whatever disaster or disease may come, and when a prayer or plea is made by any of your people Israel—each one aware of the afflictions of his own heart, and spreading out his hands toward this temple—then hear from heaven, your dwelling place. Forgive and act; deal with each man according to all he does, since you know his heart (for you alone know the hearts of all men), so that they will fear you all the time they live in the land you gave our fathers. (1 Kings 8:37-40)*

The word "plague" is one of the great terror words of the language. Since the dawn of history, this word and all that it connotes has stalked the horrified world. In its less horrible forms—what is called in this passage blight or mildew—the plague sometimes strikes nature.

When I was a boy in the hills of Pennsylvania, we had chestnut trees everywhere—from the little saplings on up to the great majestic adults. Every fall, about the first frost, the squirrels would go up and cut down the ripe chestnuts. And country boys would go out with a basket and gather them up and bring them in. They didn't ask the squirrels; but they took advantage of the busy labors of the squirrels. If there were no squirrels about, they knocked them down with rocks or plugs and then broke open the great spiny outer shell and got to the chestnuts themselves. Only a few years passed and the chestnut blight struck that state—every chestnut tree died. I'm not very good at statistics, but I remember hearing that there were only seventeen chestnut trees left out of all the millions that once graced every landscape and every meadow and every forest and field throughout that great state.

In Chicago and many other areas of the country we have the American elm. You may be familiar with that tree. It is a tall, majestic, sweeping tree that grows up like a fan. They plant them down both sides of an avenue and after a few years they come together at the top, and driving down that street is like driving down the aisle of a cathedral. But the plague has come to the elm tree. The government is fighting hard to stop it, but the elm trees are dying. And unless modern science can stop this plague, it will be only a matter of two or three more years until Chicago, that leafy forest city, will stand stark and barren because the elm trees will all be dead.

That's the plague in its least terrible form. But the full horror of the plague strikes human beings, such as in the "Black Death" of the fourteenth century. As I remember the statistics—again, vaguely—twenty-five out of every one hundred persons of the population died of the black plague. Even now, with all our antibiotics and other wonderful remedies, the words "bubonic plague" still have a grossly fearful sound in the ears of the people.

In the Bible leprosy was called a plague. A man would be living a normal life, not knowing anything was wrong with him, going to work in the morning and coming home in the evening and having his children run to grab hold of him and laugh and talk as he came up the walk. One day he notices something on the back of his hand and thinks nothing of it. "It's an insect bite," he says. But it's there the next day and the next. He doesn't tell his wife but goes to the priest, in those Old Testament times. The priest looks at it, tests it, gives it the seven-day test, and says, "It's leprosy."

Imagine the shock and horror of this terrible thing! It isn't any wonder that people hate to go to doctors if they suspect they have cancer. They don't want to hear this plague of the flesh. But this is not the worst thing that can happen to anybody, and it's not the worst kind of plague there is.

Solomon, in his prayer by the Holy Spirit, says, "each one aware of the afflictions [plague, KJV] of his own heart." Here we have the plague of the *heart*, not of the flesh; it's deeper in. It's in the spirit of the man—far in—in that part of him with which he's going to have to live forever. It's the plague of the heart.

## The Plague of the Heart

The plague of the heart is more dangerous than Satan. Satan can only destroy that which has the plague in it. He cannot harm a man without the plague. If a man has a plague in his heart, that's Satan's invitation. And it's through that that Satan gets at the souls of men. Jesus said, "The prince of this world is coming. He has no hold on me" (John 14:30b). But when the prince of this world came to Peter he found cowardice. And when he came to Judas, he found love of money. He found the plague in those two men and he ruined one and almost ruined the other. Satan is destructive only when he has somewhere to work, something that belongs to him. He is the father of all plagues. And when he finds his children in the heart of a man, he claims his children. He claims the plague spot as his own and works there. This disease is more dreadful than any physical disease, war, the calamities of nature, more dreadful than the atom bomb.

The plague of the heart can destroy the whole man. The atom bomb can pulverize you, and instantaneously you're gone; still, it can't get at your soul, your heart or your spirit. But the plague of the heart is already in the spirit, soul and heart of a man, so it is worse than the bomb, worse than any calamities that nature can visit. The plague of the heart can destroy a man.

And the strength of this plague lies in its stealthiness. It's like a panther. It has protective coloration and it can sneak up on you. It can take over unsuspected. It can lay its deadly eggs under the leaves of the Garden of Eden and there it can incubate and suddenly it appears and spreads and bursts out into the open, into ruinous conduct and habits.

And the strange accompaniment of this plague of the heart is that hardly anyone will admit its presence. Few are willing to admit that there's any plague there because it carries shame and fear. If you have an altar call and say, "Do you want to get your need met?" anybody will come because you don't lose face when you come to the altar to get a need met. But if you say, "Do you have a plague spot that you want to be delivered from?" we tighten up. You don't have many successful altar calls talking like that.

No one likes to hear about the plague of the heart. They want to laugh or be entertained with oratory or be told stories. Hardly anyone knows the plague of the heart. But there is no help possible until we know—that is, until the Holy Spirit has made it plain.

It's in the Scripture passage at the start of this chapter—when people turn and spread out their hands and confess, then they are delivered; but they don't do it till they know. Nobody visits the doctor until he has reason to believe that he's sick. Nobody goes to the blood for cleansing until he knows that he is ill—that he is unclean, that he has a plague. Only God can stop a plague; nobody else can.

The terrible thing about the plague of the heart is that you can't get to it. No surgeon can cut it away, no psychologist can probe it; nobody can get to it.

You can't x-ray it; you can't find it by any tests. There isn't anything that you can do. The plague of the heart goes deep into the nature and you can't get at it. Nobody can help you and you can't help yourself. If you're struck with the plague, you can't get to it—but it's there! It lies there incubating. Maybe it isn't very large yet, but it's growing, hatching, developing, getting into the bloodstream, into the life.

There's no help possible except God and God alone. The old writers called it "the cleansing of the forgiving love of God." I like that expression. They also talked about "the restoration of moral innocence." You know you've sinned, but you've been so completely cleansed that you feel as if you haven't. You know you have and you're penitent for all your past; but the cleansing is so complete that it leaves you like a child again, like a baby again, naked as the day you were born, innocent by the forgiving love of God and the cleansing of the blood. But the danger is that we don't know we have this plague. Look what it has done to people.

## Its Effect

Look what it did to Cain (Genesis 4:1-11). Do you think that Cain was altogether bad? Eve and Adam didn't know he was. They didn't expect a murder to take place; there was no indication of it. Don't you think Cain often picked up his younger brother and carried him about, perhaps slept close to him for warmth and gave him toys to play with? Don't you think Cain had some normal human affection? Certainly he did; but he had a plague spot and it hatched on him. John says that Cain "murdered his brother. And why did he murder him? Because his own actions were evil and his brother's were righteous" (1 John 3:12). He was jealous!

It was jealousy in the heart of Cain that caused him to say to his brother, "Let's go out to the field" (Genesis 4:8) and they took a walk, but one came back and the other was buried under the leaves. They found his blood there in the soft earth; and that blood cried to God for vengeance against the man with the plague spot.

Then there was Achan in the Old Testament (Joshua 7). Achan was a decent fellow; nobody can tell me otherwise. He had a wife whom he no doubt loved. He had a family—quite a good-sized family—and he was a good, decent, obedient man. He was so obedient and decent that no one dreamed he was the one that stole the golden wedge and the Babylonian garment, disobeying God's direct command.

If Achan was a delinquent or a borderline criminal or a fellow you had to watch, they would not have had to draw lots to find out who it was. They would have known. They would have said, "Well, there's no question it was probably him. He's been into everything; he's probably the one." Achan was a good guy; he may have sung in the choir and helped around and done lots of nice things. There was nothing wrong with Achan except that he had a plague spot that he didn't know about. He wanted gold and a garment and he disobeyed God to get

them. And when Israel was defeated God said,
"Hunt out the man with the plague spot. And when
you find him, get rid of him and you'll be all right."
So they did.

Do you think Achan ever meant to be killed or
cause his wife to be killed just because he stole a little
bit? I'm sure his face turned deathly pale when they
came to stone him. And he took his wife and put his
arms around her and I suppose he said, "Can you
forgive me? I never meant to hurt you or the
children. I just wanted the gold." I don't know what
she or the children would say or could say. But they
put them there in the Valley of Achor and stoned
them to death and put a pile of rocks over them that
all generations might see what the plague can do to
a man's heart when he hasn't dealt with it.

Then there was Herod, who used to listen to John
the Baptist (Mark 6:14-28). He'd send for him and
say, "Preach to me." And John the Baptist would
come in and preach to him. Herod was, I suppose,
an average king, and he listened with a mixture of
pleasure and worry. He had an anxiety about this
prophet. Then one evening, Herod put on a party.
He had a girl dancing for him there—one of those
pretty little painted dolls, slick and sleazy. And she
stood up there and gave it all she had and danced
before him. And the old man's eyes began to shine
with a light that shouldn't be in an old man's eyes.
And when that girl sinuously waved like a willow
in the wind and leaped and made eyes at him, he
couldn't take it any longer. He called her over, sweat
breaking out on his lecherous brow. And he said,

"What would you like, honey? Ask me anything and I'll give it." She said, "I'll ask Mama." And she dashed off and her mama was ready. She returned and requested, "The head of John the Baptist!"

Because he had made that vow before all the rest, he couldn't take it back. And so trembling with superstitious fear, he sent an executioner out and brought in the head of John the Baptist on a tray and gave it to that little wench and she took it and gave it to her mother. Do you think that Herod ever expected this? His lust and his recklessness and his fear and his pride and his love of his job—do you think he ever meant to kill a prophet? The terror might have followed him all the rest of his days because when Jesus came into his neighborhood and did miracles, he went white with fear and sent somebody out to ask if this was John the Baptist come from the dead. The ghost of John the Baptist's head grinned out of every hedgerow in the dark from that time on till Herod died. Herod never meant to do this; but he didn't know the plague of his own heart.

Later on, there was a man by the name of Ananias (Acts 5:1-10). He loved money and loved his good standing with the congregation. He wanted to give the impression that he was a generous giver, but at the same time he wanted to keep something back. So he was a liar and a deceiver as well as being a lover of money and a good reputation. He got into a tight spot and he couldn't get out. So he tried to get out by cheating and lied to the Holy Spirit.

Ananias must have had some good in him; he and his wife could stand in the fellowship of that strict early Church, which was straight-laced morally, with the Holy Spirit upon them like flames of fire. Do you suppose that he was a careless man? Never! A careless, loose-living man couldn't have gotten away with it. You think that he didn't live a close life? He certainly did. But he had a plague spot in his heart. The plague was there. The plague was on him and he lied to the Holy Spirit.

Peter said, "Send for the man." If Peter hadn't had the gift of discernment, they would never have known! He would have lived and died an old man and probably when he got old, they would have given him some kind of a Christian medal to say, "To Ananias for his long faithful work here as a member for our Lord." The Holy Spirit got through to Ananias. He had a reputation for being a prime member of that church, but he was a sneak and deceiver. He had a reputation for being generous, but he lied about how much he gave. And he fell dead and they carried him out. When they saw his wife come, she fell dead and they carried her out.

There are sins from which you cannot recover. There are sins you cannot pray for, at least one. And there are many sins that people never do because when they've committed them, they don't try to come back. They could, but they don't try to.

## It Lies Unsuspecting

The plague lies unsuspecting like the plague of lust. A man can work hard and sweat out a ministry and never know that there lies in his heart un-detected, uncorrected and unpurified the plague of lust. And the next day, it may be in all the papers. There is pride that lies in the human breast and we don't know it's there; but it lies there and incubates. Do you remember one other Herod who delivered a speech and they called him a god and he died of worms (Acts 12:21-23)? The plague broke in the very worms that destroyed the man.

I meet a lot of people who are resentful. I know a certain preacher of a certain denomination—I've known him a long time—and resentfulness is characteristic of him. You can't talk to him 20 minutes until he is bristling with resentment at something somebody did to him. This church wronged him; the superintendent stood against him; some board member betrayed him. Resentment should never be felt by any child of God. When we're Christians, we take the cross; and the cross Jesus carried, He didn't complain about.

Then there are secret sins. Now that I'm getting to be an older man and people feel a little freer to talk to me about private things, I've had people come to me and confess things that I never dreamed people did. I'm not an innocent man by a long way and I've committed many sins that are now under the precious blood of Jesus Christ, but I didn't know that women could get into the sins that they can get into. My mother gave me my concept of womanhood and I carry that concept with me. She would never say a bad word nor think a bad thought. Though she wasn't a Christian till later in life, she lived a moral life as pure as the stoics. I got the idea that that's what a woman should be like. What a shock when I got older and found that women have let themselves go until they're guilty of sins you can't talk about. It takes doctors to talk about them.

Then there are hidden grudges. Some people have never forgiven certain others for what they've done. They say, "I've forgiven them," but they avoid them, and they prove that they are holding a grudge by avoiding them.

Some people have a temper. We blame it on our Irish grandfather or on something else; but it's a plague spot. I remember a man who had a very high spiritual testimony and became a leading pastor in his denomination. One night at a board meeting, he lost his temper like a mule driver and after that, nobody believed in him.

One time, a man I thought was a fine Christian had a new car and somebody came along and dented his fender. He blew like a little bomb. I never believed in him again. Whenever I see a man blow his top, I never believe in that man unless I know he has gone to the Fountain that cleanses and gotten delivered. No man has any more right to go around with an uncleaned temper than he has to hold a rattlesnake in his jacket pocket. He has no more right to do that than he has to leave untreated a cancer on his tongue, because it will destroy his ministry. He can pray and testify, give and labor, but if one day he blows up, nobody will believe in him after that.

And there is envy. You know the difference between jealousy and envy? Jealousy is the pain you feel when you think somebody has something that belongs to you. Envy is the pain you feel when you think somebody has something that belongs to *them*. There is the difference. It's fine; but there it is. The jealous man is jealous if I take what belongs to him. But the envious man is envious because I have what I have that never belonged to him.

## Healing the Plague

God can heal the plague. He heals it by blood and by fire. There is a word that has been lost from our Christian vocabulary—it's the word, "purgation," or the word "purge." We don't use it any more. We invite people to the altar to get something; but we forget that what they ought most to receive is purgation—a purging, a cleansing. Jesus Christ purges and cleanses and takes the plague spot out and fixes that in there.

I don't know what to call this doctrine I'm preaching. I don't go along with the eradicationists, so it can't be eradication. And I don't go along with the suppressionists, so it can't be suppression. So don't press me on how to classify this doctrine; I don't know. I only know that there is blood and fire and that it will take the impurity out and make you clean and keep you clean so that you'll not be in danger of having an incubation of iniquity in your spirit that'll break out on you.

> The blood that Jesus once shed for me
> As my Redeemer upon the tree,
> The blood that makes the captive free,
> Has never lost its power.

So we used to sing in camp meetings back East.

Call it what you will, and classify yourself where you will doctrinally on this subject, there is such a thing as a victorious life. The Wesleys never taught eradication, incidentally; but they did believe that you could be filled with perfect love that would kill the old evil within you. Here is what Charles Wesley wrote:

> Jesus, Thine all-victorious love
>   Shed in my heart abroad;
> Then shall my feet no longer rove,
>   Rooted and fixed in God.

> O that in me the sacred fire
>   Might now begin to glow,
> Burn up the dross of base desire,
>   And make the mountains flow!

Just another figure; but it's the same. It is the destruction of the plague spot.

> O that it now from Heaven might fall.
>   And all my sins consume!
> Come Holy Ghost, for Thee I call.
>   Spirit of burning come.

> Refining fire, go through my heart,
>   Illuminate my soul;
> Scatter Thy light to every part,
>   And sanctify the whole.

This is what we need—refining fire to fall on our hearts to kill the plague, to destroy the plague spot in our life. Some people have coddled the plague spot and made a pet out of it. Men have euphemized it, fixed it up with a euphonious name so that it doesn't sound the way it used to. You used to call it temper; but now you say you're nervous. You used to call it covetousness when it's in somebody else's heart; but you say that you look for the future.

We may rename things, but they're the same old plagues. We need the "refining fire" to "go through the heart," to "illuminate the soul," to "scatter Thy life through every part and sanctify the whole." What we need is cleansing. If I say, "Come and get," you'll come to get. But I say, "Come and get delivered, come and get freed from something." And, of course, then we lose face when we do that and we don't like it.

I preached this at one of our camps and among those that came was a young woman; and I haven't forgotten that face of hers. She knelt at the altar and God gave her what she wanted and took away what she was ashamed of. And she leaped to her feet completely delighted. She hunted up her father-in-law with whom she'd had a quarrel and hugged the old fellow and called me over. And then she walked back and forth saying over and over again, "I didn't know it could happen to me." What happened? Let's not get technical and doctrinal and divided. Let's just say the refining fire went through her heart and illuminated her soul and scattered God's life through every part and sanctified the whole. And she leaped up and said, "I didn't know it could happen to me."

I know what God can do for a man. I had a temper so bad that once, at least, that I remember, I got so mad it made me sick. I went to bed in illness. I've seen my father get so mad that he would pull a horse back on her haunches until the bit almost made her mouth bleed. I've seen my father lose his temper and get so angry that he would grab a shovel and beat the wheelbarrow in insane anger.

I had that same thing, a temper that would leap and go. And the precious blood of Jesus and the fire of the Holy Spirit has made me unlike my father—though I grew up to be like him. When I am shaving, I see my father looking at me. But my father didn't know the plague of his own heart until he was 60 years old. He was converted when he was 60 and died four years later. He had four years to walk with God before he finally went.

God can deliver you from evil habits and evil dispositional tendencies and tempers. Little Frances Ridley Havergal testified, "This experience came to me when I arrived at the place where I knew in my heart that when the Holy Spirit said, 'The blood of Jesus Christ cleanses from all sin,' He meant 'from all sin.' "

*Relationships w/ Jesus:*
*Judicial*
*Vital*
*Volitional*
*Intellectual*
*Emotional*

# CHAPTER 5

# The Deeper Life

*Therefore let us leave the elementary teachings about Christ and go on to maturity, not laying again the foundation of repentance from acts that lead to death, and of faith in God. (Hebrews 6:1)*

By the words "deeper life" I do not mean a life deeper than Scripture indicates. I do not want anything that cannot be found within the framework of the Christian revelation. I do not want anything that is added. That is why I never buy books or listen to lectures on how to wake up your solar plexus and tune into the cosmic processes. All that is extrascriptural; any of it that is good is in the Word of God and any that is not in the Word of God is not good. So I let those fellows talk to people who don't know the Word and I stay by the Word.

I am a Bible Christian and if an archangel with a wingspread as broad as a constellation shining like the sun were to come and offer me some new truth, I'd ask him for a reference. If he could not show me where it is found in the Bible, I would bow him out and say, "I'm awfully sorry, you don't bring any references with you." So what I'm talking about is not a life deeper than the Scriptures indicate; but merely one that is, in fact, what it professes to be in name.

A Christian is not one who has been baptized, necessarily, though a Christian is likely to be baptized. A Christian is not one who receives Communion, though a Christian may receive Communion, and if he's been properly taught, he will. But that is not a Christian necessarily. A Christian is not one who has been born into a Christian home, though the chances are more likely that he will be a Christian if he has a good Christian background. A Christian is not one who has memorized the New Testament, or is a great lover of Christian music, or who goes to hear the Apollo Club sing "The Messiah" every year. A Christian may do all of those things and I think it might be fine if he did; but that doesn't make one a Christian. A Christian is one who sustains a right relationship to Jesus Christ.

Christians enjoy a kind of union with Jesus Christ. Everybody sustains some relationship to Jesus Christ; just the same as everybody in America sustains some relation to Krushchev [former leader of the Soviet Union]. My personal relation is one of active hostility so far as can be possible within a Christian framework. We can't hate people, but we can hate everything they stand for, and I want it known that I do. But everybody has a relationship to everybody else, and everybody has a relation to Jesus Christ. The relation he sustains may be one of adoring faith and love; it may be one of admiration;

it may be one of hostility; it may be one of complete carelessness; but it is an attitude of some sort. A relationship of some sort exists between every human being and Jesus Christ; that is, every human being that ever heard of Jesus Christ. But a Christian is one who sustains a right and proper relation, a biblical relation, to Jesus Christ.

## The Nature of the Relationship

The Christian sustains two kinds of relationship—or rather, the union is of two kinds; it is judicial and vital. I'll explain those two words.

In Romans we have the judicial relationship everybody sustains toward Christ: "Therefore, since we have been justified through faith, we have peace with God through our Lord Jesus Christ, through whom we have gained access by faith into this grace in which we now stand. And we rejoice in the hope of the glory of God" (5:1-2). Then in the book of Ephesians, the first chapter, that very oft-quoted passage, "Praise be to the God and Father of our Lord Jesus Christ, who has blessed us in the heavenly realms with every spiritual blessing in Christ. For he chose us in him before the creation of the world to be holy and blameless in his sight" (1:3-4), and so on.

I only quote those, not to give exposition, but only to point up the fact that we sustain toward God in Christ a certain judicial relationship, just as you have legal obligations to your children. You can get in trouble with the law if you deny them. The legal system recognizes a relationship between you and your son. It is not only biological, it is judicial—you are accountable before the law not to neglect him, abuse him, starve him or run away and leave him. You've got to look after him; he's your son.

There is a relationship which we sustain toward God in Christ. It is a relationship of children to the Father; we are children of God. Because so many verses deal with that, I don't need to quote any one of them.

Then there is a vital relationship which is another matter altogether. A husband and wife have no children and decide to adopt a boy. Under the law, that boy has exactly the same relationship to that man as if he were his own son. As the legal father before the law, he is responsible to feed and educate and shelter and care for that boy till he comes of a certain age. However, the relationship is judicial, not biological, not vital; the boy did not come from the long, age-old life stream of that father. He came from another life stream and was adopted into the family. So the father has a judicial but not a vital relationship to that son.

But a Christian has a vital relationship to God and to Christ. He said, "I am the vine; you are the branches" (John 15:5a). The branch is a branch because it sustains a vital relationship. The life of the vine is in the branch and the life of the branch comes from the vine. The two are united; that is a vital relationship. A Christian is one who has been judicially, legally made a brother of Jesus Christ and a child of God. But he is more than that—he is one who has been united to Jesus Christ by the power and motions of life so that he is vitally related to Him.

That is where we begin and, in most circles, that is where almost everybody ends. Bible schools and Bible conferences and books and printing houses are dedicated to the constant repetition of the fact that we're judicially and vitally related to Christ in salvation. That is as far as we go. There are other relationships which we can also bear toward Christ and that is what the writer meant in Hebrews when he said, "Therefore let us . . . go on to maturity" (6:1a).

That is what was meant in First Corinthians chapter 3, when Paul told them that they were carnal and they ought to move on out of that carnal state into a spiritual state. There are at least three other relationships that everybody ought to bear toward Jesus Christ: volitional, intellectual and emotional.

## The Volitional Relationship — will

Our union with Christ is judicial and vital. It is that by virtue of our faith in Christ; but there is a volitional relationship too. What do I mean by that? I mean a relationship of our will to God so that every known will of God should be mine. Everything that God wills, I should will. I should not only be judicially, legally related to Him, not only vitally related to Him in life, but in my mind, in my volitional life, I should be united to Him by doing and knowing and willing exactly as He does. That is what I mean by "Let us go on."

Most Christians do not go on to make all the will

of God their will. They sing very tenderly that rather lugubrious and pretty little ditty, "Sweet will of God, still fold me closer." I like that hymn; don't get me wrong. But we can sing that and have moist eyes and yet be selfish and self-willed and not make the will of God our own. The will of God must be known and then be adopted as my will. And then I begin to sustain a relationship of will, a volitional relationship toward Jesus Christ.

How do I know the will of God? By listening to stories told by preachers? I know by prayer, by Bible study and by experience. I go to the Scriptures and I read it regularly. I go to prayer and I ask God for grace to help me to understand it.

The fourth stanza of the hymn, "Break Thou the Bread of Life," says:

Oh, send Thy Spirit, Lord,
Now unto me,
That He may touch my eyes
And make me see;
Show me the truth concealed
Within Thy Word,
And in Thy Book revealed,
I see Thee, Lord.

I believe that hymn writer knew what he was writing about. We must pray that the Lord would give the Holy Spirit as a light upon the Scriptures. If we pray and have the Spirit of God give us illumination and we read the Word of God with avidity and relish and watch our spiritual experiences, there will

*YES!*

begin to crystalize within us a will that is God's will.

I wonder if that is what Paul meant when He said, "But we have the mind of Christ" (1 Corinthians 2:16b). There is an infinite number of attitudes and relationships within the mind and heart, and these are all wrong to start with. They don't all get corrected when we get converted either. They don't all get corrected after we've been to Bible school. They get corrected only by working on them. By prayer, study, spiritual experience and the illumination of the Holy Spirit, those attitudes begin to become spiritual instead of carnal. They begin to get straightened out.

## The Intellectual Relationship — *MIND AS IT IS*

There is a second relationship that we should go on to: an intellectual relationship to Jesus Christ. Of course, there is a sense in which the volitional and the intellectual come as soon as we're converted; but there is another sense in which they wait for development and growth. By the intellectual, I mean we should think the way Jesus Christ thinks; that we should think scripturally, that we should see things the way the Lord Jesus sees them, that we should learn to feel the way the Lord Jesus feels about anything or anybody, that we should love what He loves and hate what He hates.

The question then arises, does God actually *hate* anything? Sure he does—He says so. "You have loved righteousness and hated wickedness; therefore God, your God, has set you above your companions by anointing you with the oil of joy" (Hebrews 1:9).

*JOY = FULLNESS*

It is a psychological impossibility to love anything without hating its opposite. If I love holiness, I hate sin. If I love truth, I hate lies. If I love honesty, I hate dishonesty. If I love purity, I hate filth. Hate is only bad when it is aimed against people made in the image of God or when it springs out of some unworthy or low motive like jealousy or envy or anger. We should learn to hate what Jesus hates. I'm sure that if we had the mind of Christ intellectually, so that we judged things the way He judges them, there would be less need for preaching separation from the world than there is today among Christians.

In my earlier Christian life I read a great deal of the English authors Keats and Milton. Then I got away from Keats; I still admire him very greatly for the marvelous music of his poetry, but there's nothing of God in it, nothing of Christ. So I don't find it very helpful any more. Milton, of course, is all right. I think we'll read Milton in heaven.

But here's what the critics said about these two men. Keats was an Englishman born of English stock, reared in England, and, I think, never left England, and died when he was in his twenties—an Englishman of Englishmen. But Keats had read Greek literature so much that his mind was not an English mind; it had nothing of the restrictions and strengths and weaknesses of the British mind at all. It was a Greek mind. He thought like the Greeks.

Milton was an Englishman as well, born English of the English. He lived in England all his life—perhaps a few trips abroad, but not many. He lived and

*Milton vs Keats*

died in England and is the second of all the great English poets. Milton read the Bible and memorized it so much and lived in it so much that he was a Hebrew in his heart. Milton had a Bible mind which got into everything he wrote. He could not knock off a common sonnet of fourteen lines but somewhere in it, would be the lilt and rhythm of the Hebrew melodies, Old or New Testament. Of course, I understand the New Testament was written in Greek, but it is Hebrew in its thought pattern.

Here we have two minds, both of them English, living in the same country and eating the same kind of foods and seeing the same scenery and having the same kind of basic education. And yet one of them became a Greek in everything but nationality because he loved Greece so much. The other became Hebrew, or biblical rather than Hebrew, because he loved the Bible so much.

Now that is what I mean. You can have a Christian mind, a biblical mind. You can be Bible-minded in the sense that even though you are an American, you have a New Testament mind. I believe that is what the Holy Spirit wants to do for us. I believe that He wants our intellectual relationship to Jesus Christ to become so close, so intimate, so all-embracing that we'll think as Jesus thought, and love as He loved and hate what He hated and value what He valued and have the mind of Christ in us.

This does not come by believing on Jesus and buying a Scofield Bible and singing choruses. You have to go beyond that, "on to maturity." Those things are all basically sound and right and good;

and I have no objection. Stick by your Scofield Bible. It is good. It did, since the early part of this century, wonderful yeoman service in helping us stand against liberalism and modernism; but it has its limitations. Its limitations consist of an excess of emphasis upon the judicial relationship to Jesus Christ and very little about going on to maturity. But that is the same criticism that I bring against most of evangelicalism today. So I say there's a volitional and an intellectual relationship to Jesus Christ which a Christian should go on to cultivate.

## The Emotional Relationship

Then thirdly, there's an emotional relationship—a love attachment to Christ. Do you love the Lord Jesus Christ—*really*? Now I know we sing that we do. We sing things that aren't very true sometimes. Do you really love Christ?

A half-comical answer was given to Moody one time when he inquired of a man on the street, "Do you love Jesus?" He answered, "I have nothing against Him." I think that is about as far as a lot of people go. We have nothing against Jesus, but can we say we love Him?

Find a young mother with a three-month-old baby—it may be howling with its first little tooth or grinning as it looks up at its parents—and ask her, "Do you love your baby?" You know what will happen—every inch of her face will wrinkle up into a smile. Ask the sick, weary boy sitting in a foxhole somewhere, cold and hungry and tired and weary of life, "Do you love your country?" He won't give you any cynical answer like some of our present politicians. I think he'll break down and say, "O, my God, if I only could go back home."

A missionary was in China for many years. While he was there, children were born to him and his wife. They were sent home and came by way of the West Coast to San Francisco. At every port of call the children would say, "Is this America, Daddy? Is this America?"

"No," he would say, "this is not America."

After three or four such disappointing incidents, the ship came into the harbor of San Francisco, and they saw the Golden Gate Bridge, the shoreline and two peaks with the sun shining down brightly on them. They stood on the deck and looked and the little children said, "Daddy, is this America?"

Suddenly he went all to pieces in a welter of homesickness and patriotism and love and memories and said through his sobs, "Yes, yes, children, this is America."

He didn't know how much he loved his country. He didn't know how dear her rocks and rills, her woods and templed hills had been to his American heart until he'd been shut away from there so long. The first sight of his homeland broke him up and he cried like the child that he was for a moment. Ask that man, "Do you love America?" He'll grin at you sheepishly and tell you that story. Yes, he loves America.

Do you love Jesus—*really*? It is possible to be a Christian, that is, to have faith in His power, in His work, in His atonement. It is even possible to have a vital relation to Him in the new birth and yet not have cultivated His fellowship to a point where we love Him very much. We're not finished until the love attachment to Christ has become so strong that it burns and glows and consumes.

When I read the writings of the old mystics and the devotional writings and hymn writers of the Middle Ages and later, I get sick in my heart and I tell God, "God, I'm sorry; I apologize and I'm ashamed. I don't love You the way these loved You." Read the letters of Samuel Rutherford. If you haven't, you should. Read those letters and then see how sick it'll make you. You'll fold that book shut and get down on your knees very likely and say, "Lord Jesus, do I love You at all considering that this was love? Then what have I, what have I got?"

There should be an emotional relationship to Jesus Christ, a relationship of love. "You have forsaken your first love" (Revelation 2:4b) said the Lord Jesus, and maybe that is what it means. You have allowed things to cool you off like the young husband who really loves his bride but he's so busy making a living for her that he neglects her. I wonder if Jesus might not have had something like that in mind— "You are busy for Me, you are dashing here and there in My service, but you've left your first love."

What is this Christian then who has gone on until he sustains toward our Lord a right, a scriptural, a Spirit-inspired volitional and intellectual and emotional attitude toward the Savior? He is one who has been freed from earthly loves and fears.

## *Freedom from Earthly Loves*

What do I mean by earthly love? I mean any love out of the will of God, any love that we would not allow God to take away. If you have anything in this world or anybody in this world that you would not let God take away from you, then you don't love Him as you should and you don't know anything about the deeper life in experience. For the Spirit-filled Christian life means that I am delivered from earthly loves to a point where there is no love that I would not allow Jesus Christ to take away. Be it money, reputation, my home, my friends, my family or whatever it may be. The love of Jesus Christ has come in and swallowed up all other loves and sanctified them, purified them, made them holy and put them in their right relationship to that all-consuming love of God so that they're secondary and never primary.

I want to ask you this question: Is there anything or anyone on Earth that you love so much that you'd fight God if He wanted to take them? Then you are not where you should be and you might as well face up to it and not pretend to be something you're not. Complete freedom means that I want the will of God only. And if it is the will of God for me to have these things, then I love them for His sake, but I love them with a tentative and relative love and not an all-poured-out love that makes me a slave. It means that I love nothing outside the will of God and that I love only what and who He wills that I should love. Then you can love everybody.

I think Paul loved Timothy and Silas and Titus and the rest of them with a love that glowed like a furnace. But he didn't love them to a point where he could not separate from them or where he would fight God for them. He only loved them in the margin of his heart; he loved God at the center. He loved them for God's dear sake. This is Christianity.

Does that mean that you are not to love your baby? No, it means that you are to love God so much that you love your baby in its right context. Does it mean you are not to love your spouse? No, you are to love him. But you are to love him in the right context, in right relationship.

There was a lady, a very intelligent, brilliant woman, and writer of note. She lay beside her baby who was very sick. She was trying to get a little sleep and trying to care for and nurse the baby, too. The little thing had a high fever and was really suffering and she knew it. She watched that little suffering face and after having done everything she could do to assuage its pains and sufferings, she turned away to think it over.

"When I turned away," she said, "I saw the strain and the pain in the flesh on the baby's face and the two bright eyes and I knew that baby was suffering. I turned and said, 'God, I'm through with you. You let my baby suffer like that; I'm through! I can't love a God who'll let my baby suffer!' "

She went on to become a rationalist, an unbeliever. Well, she was a poor fool and she didn't understand. And unless she changed her mind, and I don't think she did, she knows more now than she did then; for that has been a century ago. What happened there? Just this. She loved her baby more than she loved the God who created her. If the God who created her would let her baby run a fever, she would have nothing to do with Him. That kind of love is not love. That is supreme selfishness. It is the extension of her personality, the projection of her personality into that baby and it is sheer pure selfishness.

My own mother-in-law had a baby that died and she went through fire and water and blood and tears and toil, but through it she came to a wonderful spiritual experience. She had to sit up in bed, weak and weary as she was, and make the baby's coffin. Her husband made it out of wood and she made a cloth lining of whatever she could get hold of. When the funeral was held, she stood by the grave with the rest and when everybody was expecting her to break down, she said, "Shall we sing together?" And she led off in the Doxology. Some people went away and said, "Mrs. Pfautz is insane." Others went away with moist eyes and said, "There's a faith and love that can give her newborn to the grave and sing 'Praise God from whom all blessings flow' beside that grave."

If you love anything enough that there's any question about whether God can have it or not, you know nothing about the deeper life; you are a slave to that love whatever it is. If we've been freed from every earthly love, then we have no unsatisfied longings and we have no wishes and no dreams. I never use the word, "wish," never! Years ago, I quit it; and if it ever breaks out in my speech or preaching, it is only a colloquialism, I never mean it. If God wants me to have something, I'll pray for it. And if He doesn't want me to have it, I don't want it.

## Freedom from Earthly Fears

The Christian who goes on gets freed from earthly fears. These two chains bind the whole human race: loves and fears. We love something and can't get it or we love something and we're afraid we're going to lose it. So we're bound with that chain. Or we're afraid we'll get something we don't want; we're afraid we'll lose something we have, we're bound with that chain. Fear and love bind humanity in two golden chains.

And the gospel of Jesus Christ never is finished until it goes on to set us free from loves and fears. We'll love our family more than we ever loved them before. We'll love our country with cheerful devotion. We'll love every good thing there is in the world; but we'll love it in its right context and we'll love it for Jesus' sake. And we'll hold it lightly, so we can let go of it any second for the Lord's sake. That is to be free from earthly loves.

Freedom from earthly fears means that I choose the will of God now and forever; it is my treasure, my whole attitude. The only fear I have is to fear to get out of the will of God. Outside of the will of God, there's nothing I want, and in the will of God there's nothing I fear, for God has sworn to keep me in His will. If I'm out of His will, that is another matter. But if I'm in His will, He's sworn to keep me.

And He's able to do it, He's wise enough to know

how to do it and He's kind enough to want to do it. So really there's nothing to fear.

I get kidded by my family and friends about this, but I don't really think I'm afraid of anything. Someone may ask, "What about cancer? Do you ever fear that you'll die of cancer?" Maybe so, but it will have to hurry up, or I'll die of old age first. But I'm not too badly worried because a man who dies of cancer in the will of God, is not injured; he's just dead. You can't harm a man in the will of God.

Socrates, the heathen stoic, could die saying, "No harm can come to a good man in this world or the next." If he could say it, a pagan, why should I tremble and walk softly through this world looking over my shoulder furtively? Rather should I, by the grace of God, say, "Lord, I believe at least as much as a pagan. I believe no harm can come to a good man in this world or the next."

"But I'll lose my job."

Well, you'll lose your job then; you won't lose your head.

"What if I lose my head?"

Well, if you lose your head, you won't lose your Savior. Can't harm a good man. So a good man is free from fear.

I pity the preacher that is afraid of his congregation or afraid of his superiors in his denomination. Maybe I'm a little abnormal on that, but I've never known one single twinge of fear of my superiors; and only rarely do I ever get self-conscious before a congregation. If there's somebody who really is a great preacher present and I know that my poor little sermon will sound rather amateurish by comparison, I feel a little inadequate. But nothing can harm you if you are in the will of God.

If you let the love of God burn within you until it consumes everything, then you will never be a slave to any earthly yearnings—even though you still have them. You'll have earthly yearnings and earthly loves and people you love and care for and would weep to part with; Jesus wept beside the grave of His loved friend, Lazarus. There's no harm in weeping when we must say goodbye.

Our son Wendell said goodbye last evening to fly throughout South America. He was flying out in a blizzard; I didn't like it too well, but he was breezy. He tried to pretend he didn't care. You can have your own personal loving feelings; but you are not a slave to them. You are boss of them. And you can have your dislikes; I'd run a mile to keep from having a needle put in my arm.

Once when I was ill, a heart specialist came to my house—somebody sent for him, I don't know who. He came upstairs to my room and sat down beside my bed. And when he came in, he had this huge rocket in his hand with a long sucker affair; and I saw it. And, brother, did I argue him down.

He said, "Now, I'll give you this and you'll sleep and you'll be all right. It's just a sedative."

I said, "You won't give me that."

And he said, "Well, if you are going to make so much of it, probably you'd be worse off if you took it." So he said goodbye and left. And I got better.

So I don't say that the deeper life—the Spirit-filled

life—means that you won't be normal. If lightning strikes near you, you'll jump. And if somebody comes at you with a needle, you'll shrink—you are human. But that is one thing; it is quite another thing to walk around chained by human fears—chained by the fear of death or the fear of sickness or the fear of poverty or the fear of friends or the fear of enemies. God never means that His children should thus be afraid.

All that I've preached to you now is not a dream. It is not a misty ideal that nobody can reach. It is the normal Christian life. Anything short of it is abnormal or subnormal. Shall we not obey God and go on to maturity? May God grant that together we may press on out into the deep waters, "deep enough to swim in" (Ezekiel 47:5).

# CHAPTER 6

---

## Unity That Brings Revival

*How good and pleasant it is*
*when brothers live together in unity!*
*It is like precious oil poured on the head,*
*running down on the beard,*
*running down on Aaron's beard,*
*down upon the collar of his robes.*
*It is as if the dew of Hermon*
*were falling on Mount Zion.*
*For there the LORD bestows his blessing,*
*even life forevermore.*
*(Psalm 133:1-3)*

Here painted by the pen of inspiration held by David, is one of the most charming pictures in the entire Bible. It is a picture of brethren (not men only, but men and women and young people) of united minds, met together in unity. Then because they were thus met together and because there was unity, we read about oil and dew and life and blessing. Now the coming together in unity was man's part. The pouring out of oil and dew and blessing and life, that was God's. So it is necessary for a united mind among people desiring spiritual visitation.

This text shows, as the rest of the Bible will confirm, that unity of mind on the part of the people of God precedes the blessing. I have often heard people pray, "Oh Lord, send the Holy Spirit that we may become a united people." That is all right except it is precisely backwards. The Holy Spirit comes because we are a united people; He does not come to make us a united people. Our prayer should be more like, "Lord, help us to get united in order that the blessing might flow and there might be an outpouring of oil and dew and life." That's the way we should pray.

If you look at the book of Acts, you find in the second chapter that

> When the day of Pentecost came, they were all together in one place. Suddenly a sound like the blowing of a violent wind came from heaven and filled the whole house where they were sitting. They saw what seemed to be tongues of fire that separated and came to rest on each of them. All of them were filled with the Holy Spirit. (2:1-4a)

And then a few months later, they prayed again, and

> After they prayed, the place where they were meeting was shaken. And they were all filled with the Holy Spirit and spoke the

word of God boldly.

All the believers were one in heart and mind. No one claimed that any of his possessions was his own, but they shared everything they had. (4:31-32)

The assumption is they had been like that right along. They didn't get that way because the place was shaken where they were assembled. The place was shaken where they were assembled and they were all filled *because they had been that way*. It doesn't say they *became* of one heart. It says, "All the believers were one in heart and mind. . . . With great power the apostles continued to testify to the resurrection of the Lord Jesus, and much grace was upon them all" (4:32-33).

## Unity Brings Revival   *Unity of Spirit*

This teaches us that unity is necessary to the outpouring of the Spirit of God. If you have 120 volts of electricity coming into your house but you have broken wiring, you may turn the switch, but nothing works—no lights come on, the stove doesn't warm, your radio doesn't turn on. Why? Because you have broken wiring. The power is ready to do its work with all the appliances in your home, but where there is broken wiring, you have no power. Unity is necessary among the children of God if we are going to know the flow of power.

In the book of Philippians, Paul says,

If you have any encouragement from being

united with Christ, if any comfort from his love, if any fellowship with the Spirit, if any tenderness and compassion, then make my joy complete by being like-minded, having the same love, being one in spirit and purpose. Do nothing out of selfish ambition or vain conceit, but in humility consider others better than yourselves. Each of you should look not only to your own interests [that is, your own advantage], but also to the interests of others. (2:1-4)

Revivals, whether big or small, have been mainly this: the achieving of a oneness of mind among a number of Christians. There is much isolated blessing these days that falls short of this. Revival, you see, is a persistence of the spiritual mood. We all have times of spiritual moods and there are occasional times in churches when a sudden spiritual mood comes among the people of God. But a revival is a persistence of that mood among the people that carries over from day to day and from week to week. This persistence enables the Holy Spirit to do what He couldn't do if it were broken. The average church is like this: We come on Sunday and we get a little blessing and we lose it until Wednesday. Then we come and get another little blessing and we get back up the peak and then we lose it till Sunday and then we get back on another peak. It's a continual going up to the peak and down into the valley and back to the peak again. Now it's better to do it that way than not to do it at all. But it's a whole lot better to stay on a high level than to come down in the middle of the week and have to come to a prayer meeting to get back up. Prayer meetings are necessary and you should come, but not to heal up your broken wires. We ought to stay one; the mood, the spirituality ought to persist.

I've talked about a oneness of mind and I must make clear what I mean by it in order that you might not misunderstand me. I am not referring particularly to identical doctrinal views. Probably, it would be impossible to achieve them. You see, a Protestant church is like a democratic society, and I believe it ought to be that way.

## An Example from Government

There are two kinds of governments now in the world. The democratic society is one. In a democratic society everyone is free to have a variety of opinions—and we usually do. But when the chips are down, when the need arises, we stand together. In the United States in 1941, there were divisions everywhere; everybody was after everybody else— and then the Japanese bombed Pearl Harbor. It united the country overnight. The news of that bombing brought them together and Democrat put his arm around Republican and Republican and Democrat put their arms around the middle-of-the-roader and they were united till the war was over. Then they went back to slugging it out again.

It's the same all over the world. Canadian Conservatives quarrel with Canadian Liberals. I hear over the radio how they fight; you would think they were scoundrels and ought to be in jail, but they don't mean it at all. Just let someone declare war on Canada, and they would be one in a second—everyone from the traffic cop on the corner to the prime minister would be united. I believe you can have differences of opinion and yet be united because differences of opinion are incidental, but unity is fundamental.

There is another kind of government in the world—the totalitarian government. There you are united because you have to be. If you have an opinion, you don't dare whisper it, or somebody's likely to turn you in to the gestapo. So everybody's united. And when they have an election, everybody votes for Khrushchev because they'd rather vote for Khrushchev than to go to Siberia and dig in the salt mines. So everybody votes the same way. They are united, but only out of fear and intimidation and brute force.

In the Catholic Church everyone is united. There is very little place for difference of opinion at all because they tell you what to believe. You either believe it or you cannot be saved. When something has become a dogma, it is necessary to salvation and you either believe it or else you're out.

In most Protestant churches it's quite otherwise. There are certain great basic truths that we stand for and that we believe are necessary to salvation, but on the nonessentials we exercise tolerance.

## An Example from Biology

I know of one analogy that is rather grotesque and

maybe even a bit silly, but it is at least illuminating. What is necessary to our lives and what must we all have? We must all have a heart and it must beat so many times per minute. It can vary a little, but it dare not vary much. And we must all have lungs for the getting of our blood purified by oxygen. And we must all have a brain and mind. We must all have a spine and nervous system. And there are certain other organs we must all have—the tallest, the shortest, the oldest, the youngest—we must all have them.

However, there are certain things you can take away from our bodies and they can still function. You can cut off a man's hand or leg and he can make do without it for the rest of his life. You can take a lot away from a man and he's still a man and can still think and talk and do anything that he could do before. But there are certain things you can't take away. If you take them away, he dies. Cut out his heart and he is dead. Cut out his lungs and he is gone. Let his blood leave his body and he expires. Let his kidneys stop functioning and in a few hours they will be wheeling him to the morgue.

So in the Church of Christ there are the great organs of truth, great organs that must function or you don't have a Church.

> I believe in one God, the Father Almighty,
> Maker of Heaven and earth, and of all things
> visible and invisible;
> And in one Lord Jesus Christ, the only begot-
> ten Son of God, begotten of His Father before

all worlds, God of God, Light of Light, very
God of very God, begotten not made, . . . who,
for us men and for our salvation, came down
from heaven, and was incarnate by the Holy
Spirit of the Virgin Mary. . . . He suffered and
was buried; and the third day He rose again
according to the Scriptures, and ascended into
heaven and sitteth on the right hand of God
the Father. . . .

And I believe in the Holy Spirit, the Lord and
Giver of life, . . . who with the Father and Son
together is worshipped and glorified. . . .

These are the great organs of truth. We believe
them. We believe in righteousness. We believe in the
resurrection of the dead. We believe in the coming
of Christ again. We believe in the blood of the Lamb.
We believe in the redeeming power of that blood.
We believe in the Lordship of Jesus. We believe in
the Trinity. We believe in man's sin. We believe in
God's forgiveness.

These are the great organs of truth. You take them
out of the Church and you do not have a Church;
you only have a religious organization. Put them in
the Church and let them function and then you have
a Church indeed.

For that reason I believe that there's a place in the
fellowship of God's children for people who hold
different views on things that don't matter. Just the
same as there is a place for a red-headed man in the
Church. There's a place for a bald-headed man in the
Church. There's a place for a little short man in the

Church. There's a place for a tall lean man in the Church. There's a place for a beautiful woman in the Church and there's a place for a plain one. We don't say, "You've all got to be red-headed or you can't join this church," or, "You've got to all be named Mary or you can't join this church." We don't say, "Everybody has to be named Jack, here."

We say, "There are certain great fundamental truths and we unite on them." Then you can be short or long, tall, red-headed, black-haired or no hair. You can be whatever God has made you. That's Christian democracy at its finest. Loving each other and being one.

## What Unity Is Not

What do I mean by the unity that brings revival? First let me say what I don't mean. I don't mean the unity of fear. In fundamental circles a generation ago we had a hierarchy that was just as powerful and just as tough as the hierarchy that controls the Roman Catholic Church. Of course, they never had been elected; they just appointed themselves. And if you said anything that didn't jive with the notes of the Scofield Bible you were out on your ear, skidding across to the other curb.

Everybody had to believe exactly the same thing about everything, including the second coming and the antichrist and all the rest. Everybody had to believe exactly what everybody else believed. I grew up in that kind of an atmosphere and I was one of the first ones to rebel against it and fight it.

The oneness I'm talking about then is not the

oneness of a totalitarian church where somebody in a pulpit tells you what to believe and you all sit there and say, "Yes, sir, yes sir, yes sir." If I preach something and you search your Bible and find it isn't so, I don't want you to believe it. I want you to come to me and say, "Brother, I liked your sermon; but you were off on this." We have the Book here and that Book tests whether we are right or wrong.

Then I don't mean the oneness of passivity and compromise. In order to stay one, some churches have the oneness of passivity. Nobody cares much anyway and so they just compromise. That is the beautiful unity of the dead. I suppose there isn't anything more united than a cemetery. Everybody there, whether they were Democrats, Republicans, Tories or Patriots while they lived, all lie there calmly together because they're dead.

When you go into a church where the pastor is afraid of hurting somebody who has a large checkbook, who is careful to say nothing at all and take no position, everybody gathers around him. He is dead and he gathers a lot of dead people around him and they call that a church. It's not a church at all; it is simply a conglomeration of dead men, afraid to have an opinion. It is the beautiful tolerance of the dead.

## What Unity Is

Now, what do I mean? This is how God will revive a church and the only way He will do it: there must be among us a oneness of determination to glorify the Lord alone. The Lord will not ask if you are

Arminian or Calvinist, but He will ask, "Are you determined to glorify me alone?"

In order to have this unity, all the Lord's people are going to have to get together on this. We have to determine to glorify the Lord and not to seek honor for ourselves. I try to pray very often, "O God, bless this city today. And if you must bless somewhere else, not through me, then bless somewhere else. But bless, Lord. Glorify Thyself." I don't want God tying His blessing to me. I want God to bless any man that will meet His conditions anywhere. Whatever church it may be or wherever it is, I want God to meet His people wherever they meet His conditions.

I want to be in on the blessing and I want my church to be in on it, but I want God to understand that I'm not selfishly pleading, "Lord, bless me and my people." I want God to bless and honor wherever the people are dedicated to the glorification of the Triune God, each glad to have God use the other if He wants to do it, and no man seeking his own advantage, but the advantage of others. We must first be united in our determination to glorify the Lord alone.

Second, we must be united in absorption in the Lord's doings. Persistence of the spiritual yearning is often ruined by side interests. God wants His people to talk Christ and to think Christ and to dream Christ and to love His Word and His ways and to be so dedicated to it that the conversation normally swings around to it when they're together. And I do not believe that God can continue to bless nor send anything like a life-giving revival to a church until we are absorbed in it. To get anything done, you've got to be absorbed in it.

Nobody ever did anything when he only did it halfway. Men who have done great things have always had to be dedicated men. To make the electric light and the talking machine, Edison slept only four or five hours a night and worked constantly. To compose great musical scores, men have sat up all through the night. Tchaikovsky used to stay awake hours upon hours; when others were sleeping, he would be working. My opinion of Tchaikovsky's music is such that I wonder why he didn't just take a nap. But anyway, what I'm saying is that in order to get it done, he had to stay awake and do it. Byron, one of the great English poets, said, "I shut myself in my room and work as much as 18 hours at a stretch, never even get out to take a drink of tea." And that's something for an Englishman. So you have to be interested in something.

Professional athletes—hockey, baseball, football—are dedicated to their sport, completely sold out to it. I talked to a young man one time who convinced me that some people are dedicated bull fighters. I'd like to know why. What in the world could ever persuade a man—a creature made in God's image, with abilities to do wonders, perform exploits and leave his name for generations to follow—to dedicate his life to fighting a bull? And we Christians are called upon to be dedicated!

I recently read the words of a great Christian leader who has been around the world several times. He said, "The only religion that I have found in the world that people don't take seriously is Christianity. The Buddhists take themselves seriously. The Mohammedans take themselves seriously." But the Christians play at it too much. We have the one truth that would save the world and we're the ones who play like children in the marketplace (Luke 7:32). We've got to be absorbed in the Lord's doings.

3. Third, we've got to be one in determination to see God's wonders. Remember, you have just as much of God as you want. And the Church has just as much blessing as it wants, no more. "Blessed are those who hunger and thirst for righteousness, for they will be filled" (Matthew 5:6). So says the mighty Word of God and it cannot be broken. If you thirst, you will be given water up to your thirst. If you hunger, you will be fed up to the point your hunger takes you. Therefore, the Church as a congregation of men and women and young people, we have as much of God as we really want. We've got to be united in determination to see God do His wonders. I'd like to see God break out and break over and do some wonderful things for His people. I'm not a divine healing evangelist, but I'd like to see God lay His hand on some of our sick and restore them to health again. I'd like to see God do some things the like of which aren't done in the average church.

4. There must be a unity of prayer for God's outpouring. Praying is God's method of getting things done on earth. Jesus said, "Everything is possible for him who believes" (Mark 9:23b), and also said, "All things are possible with God" (10:27b). Prayer

unites God and the praying man in one and says God is omnipotent and the praying man is omnipotent (for the time being), because he is in touch with omnipotence.

I see an awful lot of unbelieving humility and constant self-reproach—apologetic, timid and afraid. We dare not be. "Let us then approach the throne of grace with confidence [boldly, KJV], so that we may receive mercy and find grace to help us in our time of need" (Hebrews 4:16). So let's come boldly. Shouldn't we be humble? Certainly we should. But no man should be so humble that he doesn't ask, or we're playing into the hands of the devil. We should be humble; but we should dare to ask and seek and knock.

There must be expectation. We've got to point up our prayers. I have said it before and repeat it, that one of the greatest snares in praying is to pray vaguely. I used to go out rifle shooting in the state of Pennsylvania. I still like to when I get out that way. I used to enjoy using a big gun, like an eight millimeter or a 30-30, because the thing would go "Boom!" and the smoke would fly and I'd almost fall over and I felt really big. But if I'd been shooting at something, I was red-faced because I'd usually miss it.

And when a man prays vaguely, he makes a big boom and others say, "Oh, he is a praying man." But what is he praying about? Has God heard his prayer, or is he just shooting at a cloud? How do you know if he hits it or not? He is shooting at the side of a barn. Maybe he hit it and maybe that's just a knothole you say, "No, I didn't hit it. I'm sorry." If I pray for something and God doesn't give it, it doesn't do God any honor for me to make myself believe I have it.

You want to be filled with the Holy Spirit, and you say, "All right now, I'll take it." That's what you think. You ought to be willing to let God test you and know whether He's answered your prayer or not. Well, you've got to expect.

5. We also need oneness to submission with our Lord in our midst. By this I mean the fusion of our minds into a way for the Lord, the making out of many minds a beautiful mosaic highway for the chariot of God. It means being one in our resolution to put away forbidden things.

6. Moral standards are pretty low in modern evangelical circles, I regret to say. We smile and shrug at things that people used to be horrified about. We'll never have much of a revival until we have united to put away things that are forbidden—public and private differences and personal sins. If there are public differences, they must be publicly made right. If they're private differences, they can be privately made right. But we've got to be one. Not one, I repeat, as in the cemetery because we're afraid to think, but one in these determinations to glorify the Lord in our midst.

It says in Psalm 133 that because they were united and dwelling together in pleasant unity, it was like the precious ointment upon the head that ran down upon Aaron's beard, down to the skirts of his garment. God poured the Holy Spirit on Jesus Christ; He didn't baptize Him with the Holy Spirit, He

*BAPTISM VS ANNOINTING*

He didn't baptize Him with the Holy Spirit, He anointed Him, there's a difference. Jesus was never baptized with the Holy Spirit; He was anointed with the Holy Spirit. When He was anointed the oil came in such great profusion down over His head and ran clear down over His body.

And just as Aaron's body had the oil dripping down around it, dripping onto his clothing, so that he smelled like the oil that had been put on his head, so this living together in unity among the Lord's people brings a blessing of oil, an anointment that comes down upon us. It's the same ointment that ran on the head of Jesus, even the Holy Spirit, and comes down all over His people. You and I are members of that Body of which He is the Head and the oil that flowed on His head can flow down over His Body which is you and me, and we can keep an unbroken continuity of life from the Jordan River. The life of the Holy Spirit came upon the head of Jesus and it comes now upon you and me and upon all the people of God that dwell together in unity.

Are we such that God can bless us? Do we have this unity of determination to glorify the Lord alone, of absorption in the Lord's doings, of a determination to see the Lord work, of oneness in present expectation, of submission to the Lord and of resolution to put away everything that hinders? If we are, then we're a united people and we may expect any time the oil that flowed on the head of Jesus to flow down over us and bring oil and blessing and life for evermore.

# CHAPTER 7

---

# Five Rules for Holy Living

*Show proper respect to everyone: Love the brotherhood of believers, fear God, honor the king. (1 Peter 2:17)*

I don't know whether you live by principles and rules or not, but I tend to. I don't like to live "off the cuff" or "play by ear" all the time. I like to have a score before me so I know where I'm going.

When we come to living in this complex world—the only one we hope to live in before we live in that grand world of God above—we ought to get hold of certain great principles. A great principle changes your whole life; it's a nail in a sure place, something to build on, something to steer by, a beam to fly on.

Therefore, I give you five principles here to live by. If you take them and put them into practice, you will find that they stabilize your life and make you bloom and blossom and grow.

## Venerate All Things

The first principle is *venerate all things.* God made the world; it is a beautiful thing and something to venerate. It's a great loss—a tragic loss—that we've suffered in the last generation. We have lost the ability to wonder. We know so everlasting much and we're so sure of ourselves. But David stood and wondered in the presence of God's creation; he raised his eyes and said, "What is man that you are mindful of him?" (Psalm 8:4a). And Isaiah and Jeremiah and Ezekiel and all the rest of them stood and wondered in the presence of God Almighty's creation.

The Old Testament is a rhapsody on the natural creation. Have you ever noticed that 104th Psalm? The psalmist begins with praise to God, then goes on to talk about God laying the waters and making the clouds His chariots and walking upon the wings of the wind. The birds, the hills, the goats, the rocks, the conies, the moon and the seasons, the sun and the darkness, the beasts of the forests, evening and morning, earth and the wide sea—all this the man of God talks about there in a wonderful rhapsody of delight with the creation.

Everything is a bright miracle. It's not only a miracle when Christ turns water into wine; it's also a miracle when the sun rises with its healing rays and drives off the fog and brings out the bud and brings the frog out to croak in the grass and the fish to swim and the bird to whistle and sing in the air. All God's handiwork is a wonderful miracle. If we only knew it, we would find that we are living in a world that is not a broken-off, lost, dark no-man's land. It is the back door of heaven, and if we listen we can hear the angels sing.

The footprints of God are everywhere about us. And while we can't see Him, we can see His luminous trail like a bird that sings while hidden in a tree. As Middleton said, "The bird sings darkling." We can't see the bird, but we can hear her sing. God sings among His branches and sings in His universe. You and I cannot gaze upon Him, for no man can see God and live. But we can hear Him sing His song of creation and redemption. And we can feel the pressure of His breath upon us as we move through the world. We'll never see things rightly till we see them as the garments of God.

An old Englishman once wrote, "Your enjoyment of the world is never right till every morning you awake in heaven and see yourself in your Father's palace and look upon the skies, the earth and the air's celestial joys, having such a reverent esteem for all as if you were among the angels. The bride of a monarch in her husband's chamber hath no such cause of delight as you."

You live in the world that God has made. Therefore, we ought to remember that this world that we live in is a lattice through which, if we look carefully, we can at least see dimly the garments of God as He passes. We ought to learn to live like that. We've become secularized; we've allowed the merchants and the scientists to pull us down and make us secular and worldly. We ought to all be poets; we ought to all be musicians. I can't play an instrument, but I'm a musician nevertheless. And I never wrote much poetry, but I'm a poet nevertheless. And so are you and so are we all when we can see God Almighty in His world and hear the voice of God calling. We go out in the world and see nothing but God.

William Blake, the great English poet, was standing on the seashore one early morning looking out east across the waters as the sun was coming up. A man walked up and stood beside him; there came the sunrise, coloring all the eastern sky and the little waves caught the color and began to break it in a thousand shining pieces. And Blake turned and said to the man beside him, "What do you see?"

The man beside him was a merchant from London; he said, "That looks like a gold piece to me; I see a sovereign there. What do you see?"

Blake said, "I see the glory of God, and I hear a multitude of the heavenly hosts cry, 'Holy, holy, holy, Lord, God Almighty.' "

There's your difference, my brother. That's the different world that you live in—whether you live in a world where you see gold pieces in the skies and sun or whether you see the glory of God and hear the voice of the seraphim chanting, "Holy, holy, holy is the LORD Almighty; the whole earth is full of his glory" (Isaiah 6:3). Venerate all things.

We ought to learn to live like that. We ought not to allow merchants and scientists and worldly men to pull us down. If you are a merchant, don't get mad. I use merchants; I buy and sell. I sell my books sometimes, so I'm a merchant too. So don't get angry with me. Only remember that the ledger mentality, the file-card mentality, isn't what God is looking for. God is looking for men who can break out of vaults and storage chambers and billfolds and percentages and see God in His beautiful world. Venerate all things.

## 2 *Esteem All Men*

The next principle is *esteem all men*. Why am I to esteem all men? Because they bear the image of God. Though fallen and marred and ugly and lost, faith knows their true value. Faith knows that every man—any man anywhere—has the capabilities and capacities to become a Christian. And every man— even those whose minds are filled with impurities and whose hearts are considering evil and planning dark deeds upon their beds—has lying within, the capacity for mighty deeds for God and the capacity to know God.

Occasionally, art collectors will come upon an old masterpiece and will hire men who know how to restore it. And here it is, just an old cracked affair, smoky and terrible looking; nobody can see anything there but these keen, sharp-eyed men. These experts know that it's a daVinci or a Rubens, and they restore it. They know all the chemicals to use that will remove the dirt without hurting the paints. Pretty soon, shining there before them is an old masterpiece, shining as beautiful as it was the day that it was created.

So the world looks upon a man and says, "He's no good." Or we glare across the color lines at each other and say, "He's a black man; he's a yellow man; he's a red man; he's white trash," forgetting that "From one man he made every nation of men, that they should inhabit the whole earth" (Acts 17:26a). We are not looking at a black, white, red or yellow man; we are looking at a man made in the image of God who happens to have a little more or less pigmentation in his skin. He's the same under his skin with every man who lives in the world. You know what they said about the colonel's lady in "Judy O'Grady"? We are sisters under the skin. And you don't have to prick very deep till you find the colonel's lady under a maid—the same woman. We have faith in man because we know he was made in God's image.

That's why I walk around with something of a smile in my heart when I listen to all these scare fellows who are telling us that we're going to blow ourselves off the earth. They tell us that we're all going to be atomized and there won't even be anybody around to bury the atomic dust. I don't believe that for one second. I don't think it's in the Book; I don't think that man made in the image of God is going to destroy man. I think he may destroy a lot of men—blowing up cities is quite the modern outdoor sport in these last terrible days. But the human race is still going to go on because God made us and we're to esteem man—esteem them for what they can be.

There was a woman named Bluebird, who lived in Mulberry Bend in the Bowery in New York City a generation ago. She was a woman whose very life was given to the devil. She used dope; she drank; she used tobacco; she lived every way that Paul says we'll not even talk about. She was that kind of woman—a base, evil woman, and she was in jail. A

Salvation Army woman went and stood outside and told her she loved her and kept telling her. And Bluebird cursed her and drove her off, but she came back and told her again. And she cursed her some more and drove her off. And she kept coming back. Always this little woman with the funny hat and the little red band around it kept coming back.

Finally, one day Bluebird said, "You say God loves me. You don't love me."

And she said, "But I do love you."

Bluebird replied, "You don't love me; you're just doing your job. You're paid to do this—you're just slumming. If you love me, you'll kiss me." She was dirty and her hair was matted.

And the little Salvation Army girl reached through the bars and stuck her little face as far as she could through and grabbed Bluebird and pulled her dirty face up to her and kissed her full on the mouth. And Bluebird fell in a sobbing heap on the stone floor of the prison and wept her soul out—wept her soul back to her girlhood days, back to her innocency and her purity when she went to Sunday school and learned "God is love."

And there in a dirty heap, sobbing on the floor, she gave her heart to God. She was pardoned and let out of jail shortly afterward. Immediately, she joined some Christian group, I would assume the Salvation Army, and lived only about three months after her conversion. But her testimony! She went to every saloon, every den of sin and halfway house she'd ever been in, and told what God had done for her. And when she died, they said the funeral procession

was so long that the police had trouble with it.
Before, she'd been the dirt on the streets in Mulberry
Bend, but now she was a saint indeed.

Esteem all men—not for what they are, but for
what they can be by the blood of the Lamb and the
renewal of the Holy Spirit.

Godless philosophies are among us today that tell
us we're only animals. Out of these philosophies
have come the totalitarian states—Nazism, com-
munism, fascism and all the rest. But the Christian
honors human life because, as the poor, dirty picture
by daVinci or Rubens, human life has about it the
inklings and traces of immortality. When God Almighty, by His Son, Jesus Christ, takes that fallen
masterpiece and restores it, you will find shining out
of it again the face of Jesus Christ. For Christ became
a man and was flesh to walk among us.

## *Love the Brotherhood*

The next principle is *love the brotherhood*. This
means the brotherhood of redeemed souls, of
course, related by a higher life than the flesh.

You and I live on two planes—the natural and the
spiritual. We have a brotherhood of the natural. I sat
Friday noon listening to what I had sarcastically
called "the coronation" [the inauguration of John F.
Kennedy]. I confess I had a hard time fighting back
tears. My flesh is American.

But there's something grander and higher and
nobler than that—a brotherhood in the Spirit. I find
among Christians of all nations a closeness, a warmth
that I do not feel even for my fellow Americans—un-

less, of course, they're Christians. The person that sits beside you in the pew may be a stranger to you and only wandered in here, as we say, "a visitor to the church." But if that person is a Christian, he is closer to you than your unsaved brother, nearer to you than your unsaved father, nearer than any relative you have if they're not saved. I have relatives who are saved and they're very near to me, of course. And I have relatives who are not saved, and I have very little to say to them after a half hour of discussing old friends and old times on the farm in Pennsylvania. But I never run out of something to say to God's children—never! God's children have eternity to talk about these things. "Then those who feared the LORD talked with each other, and the LORD listened and heard. A scroll of remembrance was written in his presence concerning those who feared the LORD and honored his name. 'They will be mine,' says the LORD Almighty, 'in the day when I make up my treasured possession. I will spare them, just as in compassion a man spares his son who serves him'" (Malachi 3:16-17).

The brotherhood of the saints is a sweet, wonderful brotherhood. And they can rule me out, but if they're Christians, I take them in. How does that little poem go?

He drew a circle that shut me out—
Heretic, rebel, a thing to flout.
But Love and I had the wit to win;
We drew a circle that took him in.
(Edwin Markham)

I remember one time in Chicago we ran out of room for Sunday school. There was a Lutheran Church across the street, and we rented their Sunday school. We finally overflowed that and asked them if we could rent their upstairs church—the auditorium, as we call it. And they met and sent back the word, "We are sorry that we cannot permit non-Lutherans in the sanctuary."

We took it all right with a wry smile, and we stayed out of their sanctuary. But they don't fool me. If they're real Christians, I'm in; they can't shut me out. Their session or senate or whatever they call it voted us out, but they can't vote us out; nobody can. I go occasionally through big cathedrals here and there, and always there's one little holy spot and a sign saying, "Visitors will kindly not cross these ropes." But there are no holy spots that I cannot enter, for the Scripture says, "Therefore, since we have a great high priest who has gone through the heavens, Jesus the Son of God, let us hold firmly to the faith we profess. . . . Let us then approach the throne of grace with confidence, so that we may receive mercy and find grace to help us in our time of need" (Hebrews 4:14, 16). So I can enter the Throne of Grace and there's no holier place than that.

Any Christian is my brother, even though he may stare down his nose at me and consider that I'm not a Christian. If he's a Christian and I'm a Christian, some day I'll grab his hand in glory and say, "I told you so. I told you so. I made it by the blood of the Lamb. I made it!"

I remember once down in West Virginia where I

took my first pastorate we had a dear old saint by the name of Brother Breakiron. That's an awful name for a man as gentle and tender as he was—one of the kindest, godliest men I ever knew in my life. He had a face that shone like the morning sun, freshly polished. And his prayers and testimonies were something to hear. Well, I was talking to a man who said, "I don't believe that anybody is saved until they have been immersed."

I said, "Well, I can't argue with you; but I'll ask you one question. What about Brother Breakiron? He's a Methodist and he's only been sprinkled. Do you think he's saved?"

And this fellow rubbed his chin and said, "I don't want to say. I really don't know." Here was a dear old man, all you had to do was snip his shoelaces and he'd have gone to heaven. But this fellow ruled him out on a doctrinal technicality. You can't do it, friend; you might as well stop. You can't shut out any of the children of God on a doctrinal technicality. Love the brotherhood.

## 4. *Fear God*

The fourth principle is *fear God*—God the Father Almighty, Maker of heaven and earth, and His only Son, Jesus Christ and the Holy Spirit, the Comforter. This fear is not "be afraid of"; it means "astonished reverence." It may be anything from the fright of the guilty soul to the awestruck worship of the trembling saint.

The key to the right understanding of existence is theological. By that I mean that before we can understand anything rightly, we have to begin with God. Things can be seen in focus only when we look at them from the sanctuary. If you're outside the sanctuary, trying to find a hidden key, you'll never find it because it is God that made heaven and earth. And the word "theological" comes from the Greek word for God—*Theos*—and it is God that gives meaning to everything. Therefore it is proper and right to say that the key to the right understanding of existence is theological.

I said once in a service where I was preaching that all problems were theological at bottom and could not be solved without an appeal to theology. And right after the service, a young girl came down to the front, I would assume a high school girl. Her father was with her; he was a very brilliant chemist, involved in high-level secret research for the government. She said to me, "Pastor, I heard you say that all problems had to have theology in them before they could be solved properly. How could you solve a mathematical problem by an appeal to theology?"

Her father stood smiling beside her, and said in my defense, "Mathematics requires honesty. You've got to be completely honest to come out right in your mathematical problems. And the pastor is right that the doctrine of complete candor and utter honesty must appear even in mathematics."

Well, mathematics is not exactly my field. I'm in higher mathematics when I get up to $3.98. But I was glad to have that explanation and that defense that even a mathematical problem had to have an honest man working it or it would come out wrong—and honesty is a part of theology.

Philosophy tries to find out the reason for things and to get at the riddle of existence. And they try it by searching—philosophers try it by searching into their own heads. There really isn't too much in our heads, and since philosophers are compelled to stay within the confines of their own craniums, the result is, of course, disappointing. They never get at the real reason for existence because they're hunting around in their little dark skulls with a flashlight and they don't find very much. So philosophy has never been able to give us the real answer to life's questions.

Science, in our day, has taken over and displaced philosophy—and theology, for that matter—and science is reason's search for knowledge in nature. Philosophy searches for knowledge in the philosophers' own heads and science searches in nature. And knowledge there is obtained by observation and experiment. But neither can the scientist understand life. The key is in God. And hence, the godly man is the true sage. The man who knows God knows the Fountain and Source of everything; he has the key that unlocks everything.

They used to have an expression they don't use much any more: "He was a God-fearing man." I like that. But they don't use it now. To go through this world—this carnal, secular, evil world where the devil swishes his tail constantly and you can feel his hot breath on your neck—and yet to go through the world being a God-fearing man is an accomplishment. I'm telling you that only God can enable us to do it. So, fear God.

## Honor the King

The fifth principle is *honor the King*. What do we mean by that? It goes back to our second principle—esteem all men. We esteem all men because of their humanhood, because they were made in the image of God. And we honor the king as a king because the king derives his royal honor from the exalted worth of the men he rules.

I believe in human government, whether it's a democracy, a monarchy or whatever it may be. But I am not fooled at all by people. A king or queen earns and gains his or her honor not from within but from the honor of the people they rule. And the philosophy of the ruler is the philosophy that says that man, whether he be a president or a king or a queen, that person, who rules over men, is in a place of high honor because men are in a place of high honor.

John Fitzgerald Kennedy swore his simple oath of office, and he now sits and looks out over a big broad desk. He's president of a great country. But he's just an Irishman and nothing more. His honor is derived from 182 million men and women made in the image of God. And that beautiful, gracious lady that sits in England and reigns as queen, beautiful as she is, she's just a woman. And she gets her honor and her glory from the Commonwealth, the people over whom she reigns. The glory of the king comes from the people and the glory of the people comes from the God who made them in His image. That's the philosophy of kings and queens and presidents, and I believe in it. I believe that we value, even honor, human government because God established it. And we honor kings and queens and presidents and rulers because God placed them there over His people.

To sum up what I'm trying to say today, we are to venerate all things because God made them and His creation is the garment of the Deity. We are to esteem all men because they are made in the image of God. We are to love the brotherhood of the redeemed because Christ redeemed them and they are of our spiritual kind. We are to fear God because of who He is and we are to honor the king because God placed him there to rule over His people whom He made in His image.

I heard two speeches last week, one by an outgoing president and one by an incoming president. And the outgoing president prayed part of his speech. He spoke—but a long part of it was a prayer. The other man mentioned God once as though God were somebody that had to, of course, be acknowledged—He's probably around somewhere, but we don't know where.

And that's the difference, my brethren. You don't have to be too brilliant if you know God. And all the brilliance in the world will not settle things if you don't know God. So we'll begin with God—we'll begin where the Bible begins, where creation and time began.

# CHAPTER 8

# Communion of Saints

*For anyone who eats and drinks without recognizing the body of the Lord eats and drinks judgment on himself. (1 Corinthians 11:29)*

It is well known that man is caught in a strange dilemma between the desire for God and the fear of Him. The longing for God is age-old. The apostle said in preaching to the Greeks that they felt after God if, perchance, they might find Him (Acts 17:27). The history of the world since man has been writing and leaving his thoughts for others to read is indicative that there is a hunger after God.

Men are hungry for God. Some go away into mountains and caves and try to cultivate an awareness and get to know God that way. Others, they tell us in India, used to make their way to wash in the Ganges River by falling flat on their faces, marking where their forehead touched the ground, walking to that spot and falling again. And, thus, taking those falls, they make their way to the Mother Ganges that they might find God.

Yet there is a fear of God that we have along with

our longing for God. In the book of Genesis, it tells us that when God appeared in the garden that Adam ran and hid among the trees of the garden and God had to say, "Where are you?" (Genesis 3:9b). God had to be the aggressor and search for Adam. When our Lord Jesus Christ appeared, Peter fell down and said to Him, "I am a sinful man" (Luke 5:8) and fled from His presence. So man is caught in the middle between fear and fascination. There is a deep fascination within him that makes him want to know God and there is a deep fear within him that makes him afraid of God.

Then there is a love of sin in man that shuts out the face of God, so that man is caught in this terrible situation. The Greeks thought that in mountains and groves and rocky peaks they would find God. So they brought heifers and garlands with flowers. If you have any Wedgwood china, you know that it contains little cameo pictures. In almost every instance those cameos are from Greek mythology. On some pieces you will see a man leading an animal up to an altar to make a sacrifice to their gods.

This idea that God is somewhere and that we have got to sacrifice and take animals to Him came down through the years. Then God brought the truth to light and swept away the errors and the fancies and the shadows and He showed what the Old Testament had hinted at and pointed to and prepared us to receive, that God should appear as a man. " 'The virgin will be with child and will give birth to a son, and they will call him Immanuel'—which means, 'God with us' " (Matthew 1:23). He said, when He had grown to manhood and was teaching, "Anyone who has seen me has seen the Father" (John 14:9b). A man—not *men*, but a *man*—is the one focal point of manifestation, and that man was Christ Jesus, the Lord; so that "where two or three come together in my name, there am I with them" (Matthew 18:20).

## Come in the Name of the Lord

When we gather for worship, we come in the name of our Lord Jesus Christ. If you bring with you a psychology of denomination, I most heartily recommend that you ask God for a cleansing from it, because we ought not to divide the children of God into imaginary divisions. They're imaginary from God's standpoint. Remember that we are a family and meet in His name around the person of Christ.

In the 13th chapter of Acts, it tells us that they met and ministered to the Lord. It wasn't the preacher who was ministering, but the people. They were there worshiping the Lord "in the splendor of his holiness" (Psalm 29:2) and met around the person of the Lord. It was at that time that the Holy Spirit said unto them, "Set apart for me Barnabas and Saul" (Acts 13:2b). The church called out missionaries and sent them out because they were worshiping the Lord. They met the conditions of New Testament worship and the Lord blessed them and smiled upon them and said they were worthy to have some missionaries go out from there. So He sent missionaries out.

They gathered unto Him as I trust we gather unto Him in our day, knowing that He is here and knowing that all Deity is present, hidden from our sight, certainly, from our grosser sight, but present. They were "all with one accord in one place" (Acts 2:1b, KJV), the Scripture said, when the Holy Spirit came upon them. We now pray "O Lord, send the Holy Spirit in order that we may be of one accord." But that's not scriptural; for the Holy Spirit did not come to make them of one accord; He came because they were of one accord. Music does not come to make your piano get in tune, it comes because your piano is in tune. It is not the music that tunes your piano; it's the tuned piano that makes your music.

The word for "one accord" is a musical term for harmony—those disciples were already tuned to each other. They were in harmony with each other. Because they were, the Holy Spirit could come and fall upon them and bring the music of the spheres to the hearts of the disciples because they were one. But they had to become one before the Spirit could come upon them and baptize them into the Body of Christ.

Let us not pray, "Oh, send the Holy Spirit that we might be one." The Holy Spirit can't come and make two deacons who don't like each other or two sisters who are jealous of each other's voices—the Holy Spirit can't come and make them one. But if they will get right, then He can come upon them. We must get right and then the Holy Spirit comes. He came because they were all of one accord in one place.

The Corinthian Christians met like that but they were guilty of a serious error. I'm a believer that while the fellowship of saints is as broad as all born-again Christians, I believe also that we ought to be very careful to hold to the faith of our fathers, to every tenent of the Christian creed. There is a movement on now to receive into the fellowship of Christians persons who do not hold the faith of our fathers.

I remember what Paul said about two men. He said that he had turned them over to the devil that they might learn not to blaspheme (1 Timothy 1:20). You know what the blasphemy consisted of? It consisted of teaching that the resurrection was already passed. They had it figured out somehow, you know, they went to the Greek original and they proved by juggling one text against another one that the resurrection was passed.

Nowadays some people would have said, "Well, it's simply a mistake. They're just mistaken, but they're nice Christians, take them in." Paul said they've got to learn not to blaspheme. It's blasphemy to teach and believe that which is contrary to the Scriptures. So I believe that we ought to have as the foundation of our fellowship a solid New Testament theology.

I cannot and I dare not teach that God laid the sins of the world on the devil as the Adventists do. I must teach that He laid the sins of the world on Jesus, the spotless Lamb of God and He bore them all and frees us from the accursed load. If I do not so teach, I'm blaspheming because I am teaching a doctrine that is not true. I dare not teach that I am saved by grace and the keeping of the law. I must teach that I am saved by grace alone without the works of the law or else I am blaspheming. I dare not teach that souls of the righteous, when they die, sleep in the earth until the resurrection. I must teach that the souls of the righteous, when they die, go to be with their Lord at the right hand of God with the Savior and come back and are reunited with their body at the coming of Christ. This is traditional historic faith of our fathers and New Testament teaching.

## Be Bold and Strong

I believe that we should be bold and strong and, if we need to, fight for the faith of our fathers once delivered to the saints. You give the devil one inch, and he'll take a mile. You let the devil's camel stick his dirty nose in the tent, and the whole hump will be in there before nine o'clock tonight. So you keep the devil out. You keep him out of your doctrine and your pulpit.

That's why for the thirty-one years that I was a pastor in Chicago, I stood with a club before that pulpit. No man could preach in that pulpit unless I knew that he was worthy to preach, morally and doctrinally. The sheep didn't know how I protected them.

In Chicago, that great center of religion, everybody wanted to talk. One man rushed down the aisle to me; he wanted to debate me about baptism. I said, "No thanks." Somebody else wanted to come in and preach about what he had seen when he was chaplain of a prison. He wanted to talk about the electric chair. He said, "I want to come in and I want to set an electric chair up on your platform." He said, "And I want to tell the story of how I saw a woman hanged and she was so heavy her head pulled off."

I wrote him a letter. It was a Christian letter that I'm not afraid to face in the day when the Lord judges the secrets of men's hearts. But his face probably turned the color of a ripe lobster when he read it! "My friend," I said, "If you've done any good among the prisoners, I'm glad. And if you have brought any comfort to any of the boys who, because of their crimes against society, had to pay the last price, I'm glad. But the idea that you could set an electric chair up on my platform and stand and tell the goggle-eyed saints gruesome stories of women whose heads pulled off is beneath the dignity of the Church of Christ."

And I added, "The fact that you can come and take an offering at the door and the awestruck and goggle-eyed saints will throw their dollar bills into your hat is proof not that you're right; it's proof of the tragic backslidden condition of the Church." I never heard from him again.

Somebody else came in with a machine that takes wastepaper and crushes it into a bale. He said, "You announce to your audiences, 'Bring all your wastepaper to church.' We'll bale it and you can sell it and have money to pay the preacher and keep the church and your missionary program going."

I said, "Mister, over there's the door. I want you to get to that door just as fast as you can. I don't want my board to know that I even talked to you. If they even found out that I'd let you even make a proposition like this to me, they'd be on my neck. In this church, we go down in our pants pocket, pull the

money up, take it out and put it silently in the plate.
That's how we get our offerings. We don't bale
wastepaper."

Can you imagine when God sent His only begotten Son, the best He had, and His Son gave His
blood, the best He had, and the apostles gave their
lives, the best they had, we'd bring God our wastepaper?

So I've built a wall of fire around that pulpit. No
one could preach or talk to any of the groups unless
he was all right. One fellow got through the screen
one time. When we knew him, he was a born-again
Christian and an evangelical. Then he'd gone off to
seminary and lost his faith—but we didn't know
that, so we were innocent. We allowed him to speak
to the young people and I was present.

He got up and smiled condescendingly down
upon us old-fashioned followers of the old-time
religion and proceeded to take the faith of our
fathers apart, one tenent at a time. He finished and
said, "Now, I'm open for questions." He sat down
and there was a silence that you could have cut with
a pie knife; nobody said a thing. The youth chairman
finally got up and said, "Will you please stand? We'll
be dismissed in prayer."

Everybody stood and we were dismissed in prayer
and this fellow hung his head and silently stole
away. He thought he was going to have a fight, you
know. He thought that we Christians were going to
get up and start working on him. But not a person
said a word. They'd been too well trained. They
weren't going to argue with a man who had lost his

faith. They weren't going to start a fuss and have a lot of hurt feelings. They just let him die. When he finally left, the chairman said, "Well, goodbye, thanks for coming"—and that ended it.

## Don't Take in Everything

I believe in the fellowship of Christians, but I don't believe in going overboard and taking in everything. The day will come when sheep will be separated from goats and I'm not throwing arms of fellowship around any goat if I know it. Let the Lord separate the goats and take care of them. I'm not condemning them nor damning them; I'm just not having them in fellowship. That's why it should be hard to become a member of a church—we don't want any goats in the fellowship. When you start letting goats in, pretty soon you have a goats' nest instead of a sheepfold for your church.

Still, I don't think that we ought to attack the goats. Some preachers, God bless them, are so anxious to maintain the faith of our fathers that they carry a club into the pulpit and beat the goats from the pulpit. I don't think it's a good idea.

One Southern preacher told me that he knew there were goats in his congregation and he decided to go after them. So he prepared a sermon in which he was going to pulverize those goats. He said, "There won't be a goat left. I'll kill them. They'll get out of here." He spent three weeks making up that sermon. It was his sermon and he emphasized the fact that the Lord hadn't anything to do with it.

"I got up there," he told me later, "and for about

an hour, I poured it on. When I was finished, there was lamb's wool all over the building. But the goats were all sitting there rubbing their hands and saying, 'Amen, brother! Pour it on.'" The goats didn't get affected. That's why I don't believe in attacking the goats from the pulpit. They don't believe the truth and they're not living right; but the saints of the Lord ought to be living right and believing the truth.

The Corinthian Christians believed the truth; but they had made one error. They did not sense the presence of the Lord in Communion. They ate and drank "without recognizing the body of the Lord" (1 Corinthians 11:29), or in other words, not knowing the Lord was present. They ate and they drank but they did it in an unworthy manner, bringing judgment on themselves because they did not realize the Lord was there.

They did not observe the Communion in a proper way. So when this sense of the Lord in the Communion was lost to the church, the church began to backslide. You'll find in Revelation 2 and 3 that their love cooled off and their moral lives degenerated and their doctrine got warped and they got a name to live but were dead. As the years went by and centuries followed centuries, because they had failed to observe or discern the presence of the Lord in the Communion, they were not having the right kind of fellowship.

You can have fellowship around a variety of things. One of our six sons used to play baseball for the Navy and was invited to play for the Boston Red

Sox and refused. "When I played baseball," he told me once, "I used to play because I liked it. I played the game and went home. But some of the other players were fanatics. They gathered around and they talked about 'rubbing the bat down to the bone'—whatever that meant—and about averages and curves and all the rest. It bored me. I wanted out of there. I like baseball but not that much."

To be a good baseball man, you've got to live for it, to have it in your blood. Those men have a fellowship; but it's rather an unworthy fellowship, I would say. It's the fellowship of sports, a fellowship of baseball and they know everybody back to Honus Wagner. I've seen a few games; but I'm not that interested.

## Christ Is the Center

Truly, "our fellowship is with the Father and with his Son, Jesus Christ" (1 John 1:3). And truly our fellowship is with the saints and with the children of God. And therefore, when we have fellowship, instead of our talking endlessly about some local affair, politics, literature, music or sports, we talk a little about it because we're naturally interested in what's going on around about us; but our big interest lies with Jesus Christ the Lord—that's where our fellowship lies. Christ is our center of fellowship. And the Church has Christ as its center of fellowship—not the pastor or the board, not the choir director or the ushers. We're all one in Christ Jesus, and no one but Jesus Christ is the center of attraction.

People have complained about institutionalized

Christianity, but I say the church is not an institution. It is more than an organization; it's an organism. It's a group of born-again people who know Jesus Christ as their Lord. And if a church is only an organized institution run by a constitution with offices of authority given to certain men, it may not be a church at all. But if it's a fellowship of the saints, a gathering of believers around the magnetic person of God's Son, then it's a church.

The Corinthians forgot that Christ was the center of attraction, and Paul had to write and rebuke them. If we're here for any other reason, then we'd better take Paul's warning: "That is why many among you are weak and sick, and a number of you have fallen asleep. But if we judged ourselves, we would not come under judgment. When we are judged by the Lord, we are being disciplined so that we will not be condemned with the world" (1 Corinthians 11:30-32). The good, patient, kindly God, even when we take Communion in an unworthy manner, is ready to forgive us that He might not need to judge us and condemn us. He judges us, but in a disciplinary way and brings us to repentance in order that He might not condemn us. And there is the difference.

Let's say two boys are playing in the backyard and one of them is yours and one of them isn't, and they get into real mischief—they decide to break all the windows in sight. They start throwing rocks and break out all the garage and kitchen windows and then start on the ones next door, and you catch them. Well now, since one boy is yours and one boy belongs two blocks down, you're going to treat them differently. You're going to say to one boy, "Go home. I'm calling your father," and to the other, "Come inside; I want to chat with you."

I know; I've done it. We had one boy, God bless him, who would get increasingly obnoxious for three months. At the end of three months, I'd take him to the basement and he sweetened up like an orange and stayed that way for about a month and a half. Then for a month and a half more, he'd get increasingly impossible. And then when it got impossible for me to endure it, we went down to the basement (it was something about the cool air down there, sort of seemed to do something for the boy!). But there's the difference—if he's your child, you love him and you're smiling underneath, really; but you're not going to let him get away with that. You're thinking of his future, so you discipline and punish him. But if he's not your boy, you send him home.

In the same way God says, "I am going to discipline you because you belong to Me. I'm sorry you're living the way you are; but I'm not going to condemn you, you're Mine. I'm going to judge you and discipline you," and that's another thing altogether. David said he'd rather fall into the hands of God than into the hands of man (1 Chronicles 21:13). He knew that God was better than man.

But I have learned the ways of God enough that I don't want to fall into the hands of God either if I can help it. I do not want the discipline of the Lord, for the Lord uses the whip in order that He might not condemn us. He does it that we might be par-

takers of His holiness. It's only the obstinate mule
that you have to whip. It's only the wild skittish
horse that you have to pull back the bit and bridle.
The well-trained animal doesn't have to be pushed
nor kicked nor whipped. And the children of the
Lord ought to be so domesticated and easy to handle
that the Lord only has to whisper to them and they
get it. They keep their consciences clean and their
lives clean; they keep right. And if they even think
a thought that isn't right, they grieve before God and
repent and get it under the blood of the Lamb. God
doesn't have to use the whip on them and He won't.

## CHAPTER 9

# The Secret of Victory

*Have mercy on me, O God, have mercy on*
    *me,*
  *for in you my soul takes refuge.*
*I will take refuge in the shadow of your wings*
  *until the disaster has passed.*

*I cry out to God Most High,*
  *to God, who fulfills his purpose for me.*
*He sends from heaven and saves me,*
  *rebuking those who hotly pursue me;*
                                    *Selah*
  *God sends his love and his faithfulness.*

*I am in the midst of lions;*
  *I lie among ravenous beasts—*
*men whose teeth are spears and arrows,*
  *whose tongues are sharp swords.*

*Be exalted, O God, above the heavens;*
  *let your glory be over all the earth.*
    *(Psalm 57:1-5)*

This was written by David when fleeing from Saul and surrounded by his foes. In that brilliant way he had of describing things, David said that he found himself among lions, men whose teeth were spears and arrows and whose tongues were as sharp swords. He was surrounded by them and they had the authority of King Saul back of them, and David had nobody but God. So David, being taught in the ways of the Spirit, did something that we probably wouldn't have thought of doing. David immediately put God between him and his enemies.

David knew that he must have the victory; but he knew if he was to have anything like permanent victory he couldn't ask God to exalt him. So he didn't say, "Oh God, I am Your king, to be successor to Saul, the sinning king. Now God, I want you to come to my rescue and crush these enemies under my feet." He knew better than that. So, he prayed, I don't know whether you'd call it a prayer or not, it's an ecstatic explanation rather than a prayer: "Be exalted, O God, above the heavens; let your glory be over all the earth" (57:5). He was saying, "Whatever happens to me, God, be exalted. Whatever these men with sharp teeth and claws and spears and arrows do to me, God, let Your glory be over all the earth. My heart is fixed on this, O God, and I will sing praise because I want You to be exalted above the heavens and Your glory over all the earth."

This is God's way of thinking, which is backwards to ours. And it deserves our attention. We need to sing about it and pray about it and preach about it until we get hold of it, for we're very slow to learn. God must, Himself, be exalted above all or else David's victory would have been a treacherous one. He would have been defeated even though he had won over his enemies; it would have been a pyrrhic victory that would have cost him too much. So he put God where He belonged, high above all, exalted above all, and then David came out all right because he put God where God belonged.

That's the little secret; I could stop right here and we would have learned one of the most important things that is possible to learn: God belongs above all. When we say we magnify God, we don't mean we make God big—you couldn't do that. God's already vastly perfect but we mean that we see Him big. And when we say that we exalt Him, we don't mean that we raise Him; we mean that we acknowledge Him to be as exalted as He is.

## An Inverted Relationship

The trouble with the world is there is an inverted relationship between God and mankind—a moral derangement. The trouble with the world and the trouble with the race of men is that we have not put God where He belongs in our thinking, in our conduct and in all our philosophies and in all our attitudes of life. There are millions who pray to God, no doubt. But the true place of God in the heart is to be learned by where we put Him when we're in trouble, where we put God when difficulties come and where we put Him at other times in our life.

I want you to ask yourself these questions:

Who wins when it's a choice between God and money, between God and ambition? A lot of young people turn to the Lord when they're in their teens and are doing fine—and then they become ambitious. They have some talent and develop it, and the world finds out and sends for them. Then they have to make a choice between following that ambition, which will take them to the world and away from the church, or following the Lord. And I think a clean 97 percent of them will follow their ambition.

Who wins when it's a question of fleshly enjoyment or doing the will of God? Out in the world God would never get a vote, but in the Church it would seem to me that God ought to get all the votes there are. And yet when it's a choice between fleshly enjoyments and God, the Church usually votes on the side of fleshly enjoyments—provided we can somehow strike a compromise and have God too.

Who wins when it's a choice between marriage and God's will? I have known or read of a few instances where men and women separate because one or the other is not a Christian. A young lady told me just the other night that she was going with a young man and there was some thought that they might hook up for the rest of their lives. But because he wasn't the kind of man he should have been, she broke it off. Now that happens once in a blue moon. But it doesn't happen very often. Usually, a young man or woman follows the Lord blissfully and happily along. They're the first one to young people's service and the last one out. They're the first one to take part and to witness and to testify and all, until they meet someone. And then God gets shunted aside while they decide whether they are to marry and who to marry. And if it's a choice between God and marriage, they marry.

And a choice between God and friends? There aren't very many people who will give up their friends for Christ's sake. There aren't many who will give up *self* for Christ's sake. So who wins when the vote is between God and these things? Usually, the other things win and God loses. And that's why we're in the state we're in, you see. The curse doesn't come causeless; neither does the blessing. We're living at this poor dying rate because we are violating the laws of the kingdom.

A young man would discover the secret of victory if, when it came to a choice between a beautiful young girl and God, he said, "Be exalted, O God, above the heavens; let your glory be over all the earth." Then the victory would come in his life. And you would find many people walking in victory if, when it comes to their ambitions, they learned to say, "God, be above my ambition. Let Thy name be above all my ambitions." God would give the victory. But God won't give it to you directly. He has to give it to you by way of the throne. We have to put God where He belongs first and then, when we do, God blesses us and gives us the victory. But if we try to get the victory unilaterally, if we try to strike out in one direction to get the victory, we don't get it.

## *Putting God Down*

The world is staggering on to no foreseeable future. We're having a mixed-up time of it because we are putting God down and putting men up. When humanism came along about a generation ago and made the human mind to be the criterion of all thought and put God down, theology ceased to be the queen of the sciences. The queen of the sciences became science itself, or humanism or sociology. Then, of course, we went down because we had not put God up. If you exalt God, God will exalt you. But if you put God down, you will go down. And the world is in the mess it's in because God has no place in the minds or hearts of the people.

The work of God in redemption is to restore this inverted order: to put God up and man down, in order that He might put man up. Now in order that He might do that, God came down—as far down as He could get. It was impossible for Him to get down any further than He got. You remember what it tells us over in Philippians—"Who, being in very nature God, did not consider equality with God something to be grasped, but made himself nothing [of no reputation, KJV], taking the very nature of a servant, being made in human likeness" (2:6-7).

He voided His reputation and that's the last thing anybody wants to do. But God could afford to do it. He took upon Himself the form of a servant, and that was very humbling. He was made in the likeness of men, and that was going down still further. "And being found in appearance as a man, he humbled himself and became obedient to death—even death on a cross!" (2:8). That's another step down, and you can't go down any further than death on a cross.

What was the end result? "Therefore God exalted him to the highest place and gave him the name that is above every name, that at the name of Jesus every knee should bow, in heaven and on earth and under the earth" (2:9-10).

So, you see, we are exalted when we have exalted God and gone down. Then God takes us and lifts us up. But when we try to climb up, it's the business of God to keep us down. "Humble yourselves, therefore, under God's mighty hand, that he may lift you up in due time" (1 Peter 5:6).

But our carnal hearts want to be exalted right away. We want to get up there now, but God says, "You can afford to wait, children. My Son went down and stayed down 33 years and then went still down further and further and further until He touched the utter bottom of all possible humiliation. And then, because He did that, I raised Him and gave Him a place at My right hand, fulfilling the text that 'Those who honor me, I will honor' (1 Samuel 2:30)."

Jesus Christ honored God even in bloody death and degradation. And because He did, God put Him at His right hand and has given Him a name that is above angels. "For to which of the angels did God ever say, 'You are my Son; today I have become your Father'?" (Hebrews 1:5a).

So remember, redemption does a lot of things for us. You and I are inclined to take the kindergarten attitude toward salvation—we think its purpose is to make us happy. That attitude is abroad everywhere; people are writing books about how to be happy—just take Jesus and you'll feel good inside. But the whole purpose of redemption is not to give you a tickle inside your heart, but to reverse the inverted order of things. Redemption puts God where He belongs—exalted to the throne—and man where he belongs—down in the dust—in order that God may, from the dust, raise man to the throne. But never, never does God raise a man to the throne except from the dust. Never does He lift him to His right hand except from the low place of humiliation.

An integral part of the message of Christianity is, "If anyone would come after me, he must deny himself and take up his cross daily and follow me" (Luke 9:23b). Let him forsake houses and home and spouse and parents and his life (Matthew 19:29, Luke 14:26). We must be willing to say, "O God, if it's a choice between You and my house or my spouse or my parents, I'll take You, God."

I'm not talking out of the left side of my ear. I know what I'm talking about; I went through this. I was seventeen years old when I was converted. My mother wasn't converted, my father wasn't and my relatives weren't. My mother was a good starchy Presbyterian and looked down on a fanatic. When I preached on the street, she thought it was terrible. She said, "Can you imagine my son preaching? And not only preaching, but preaching on a street corner?" It was a terrible thought to her. Later on when she got converted herself and saw what the

Lord was doing, she humbly admitted that the Lord had been right all the time.

But you've got to go through these things for yourself. I had to walk out on my parents—I don't mean I left the house, but I had to live in a way they didn't approve of. But the Lord saved them and it's wonderful to remember. He saved my father, my mother, my brother-in-law and two of my sisters— all because I exalted God. When the choice came between my parents and God, I took God. When it came between my friends and God, I took God. We are to exalt God above all things and to live so that His glory is exalted above the heavens. This is the ladder by which you climb to the kingdom of power and the lever by which you can move mountains.

There's a richness of inward experience that the saints have had down the years and that God promises to His children and this is the secret of it. There is a deep satisfaction to the total nature and a usefulness in the kingdom of God, fruitfulness and growth, a ravishing knowledge of the most holy God—and I repeat, it is available only when God is exalted and we are abased. Can you say, and mean it, "Be exalted over me, my God. Be exalted at my expense. Be exalted, God, and let it cost me what it will cost me"?

## Too Many Bargainers

God has too many bargainers, too many Jacobs who sit down with a lead pencil and figure, "If you will bless me, God, I will give you a tenth." And Jacob lived like that—for a long time, at any rate. He

became a better man later on after God got everything. He didn't get only the tenth; God got Jacob's
wife and children and property; He got everything.

And it was all over, and Esau was on his way to
kill him. And there was Jacob, not with his tenth
gone but with everything gone but his hide. He just
had what he was wrapped in, that's all. And there
he was on the bank of the river and he prayed to God
and God wrestled with him at night and changed
his name from Jacob.

But we tend to dicker with God and try to get an
easy way. "Lord, I want to be blessed, but I don't
want it to cost me this much. Couldn't we talk this
thing over?"

"No," says God, "we can't talk this thing over. My
rules are my rules and my Word is my Word and My
will is made known in the Word and there isn't
anything to talk over. So you come My way and you
will be blessed. Go your way and you'll lose everything."

## Exalted above Possessions and Friends

It is so simple that I can't see why the Church has
missed it. "Let Thy glory be above my possessions,
O God." Some people have $25,000 in the bank
drawing interest. You can have it and I don't mind
at all; that's not the point. The point is, if it were a
choice between giving it all up or having God's
highest will, which would you do? Most people
would seek a compromise. They'd take a little of
God and a little of what they had.

And there are friendships. Fénelon said that we

find it hard to give up our friends in order to find a Friend. "There is a Friend who sticks closer than a brother" (Proverbs 18:24). You can capitalize that. We have friends of all sorts and all degrees, some who would do anything for you and some who would grumble if they had to do anything for you, but we have friends. And we've got to give them all up in order that we might have *the* Friend.

And when we have *the* Friend, we'll have friends. The Lord never takes anything away but what He gives something better back. It's always so. I gave up the approval of my parents and the respect of my friends for a little while. They thought that I was out in left field because I was following the Lord and was down among those Alliance people. And my father said my head had been filled with things.

I lost some friends; but I gained *the* Friend and now I have friends around the whole wide world. I don't think there's an island or a continent anywhere that I don't have friends on it—and I mean friends I know, people I have talked with, prayed with, preached to and who have preached to me.

I just found out that a book of mine was published in Germany. Now I have friends over there. I gave up my little handful of friends for God's sake and now I have friends all over Germany. They tell me in India, Japan, Armenia and various Spanish countries the Lord is letting my books be distributed. And I have friends there that I've never seen. I mention that only because I want you to know that when God takes away friends, for *the* Friend, He gives friends back again—better friends than you had before. God will take away people that wouldn't do you any good anyhow and He'll give you back the best people in the world for your friends.

## Exalted above Comforts and Ambitions

God must be exalted above our comforts. If some people showed up at prayer meeting, the pastor would faint and the pianist would tumble over in a dead heap, because it's not comfortable for them to be there. I don't know what there is on Wednesday nights on TV, but that's no doubt one of the reasons. But anyhow, we need to give up our comforts. To curl up in front of the fireplace on a cold night is really something. But Jesus Christ, our Lord, got up and went out into the cold bleak world and gave His all and so did His apostles and so have the saints all down the years. So give up our comforts. "Be exalted, O God, above my comforts and my pleasures."

God must be exalted above our ambitions—all these private projects that people have. He must be exalted above our reputation. That's always a pretty hard thing to die to; we desire to have a reputation. And when we find we can't get any, we want a reputation for being happy that we don't have a reputation. That's the way it works: we find we don't rate, then we smile like St. Francis and say, "Well, I don't rate, praise the Lord." And then people say, "Isn't she saintly? She's happy because she doesn't rate." But it's another way of rating, you see. It's just another way of getting your ambition fulfilled.

And then, He must be exalted above my likes, my dislikes, my health and finally, even life itself. All my life I have had to chase away friends who were afraid I'd kill myself. They would say, "I'm afraid you'll kill yourself; you'll work yourself to death." Don't you worry about that, my brother. Working yourself to death in the kingdom of God is a wonderful way to die. But God doesn't let many of His people die like that.

Finney used to teach that if you rest in the Lord and wait patiently for Him, you won't die until you're at least seventy-plus. But he went on to say that lots of preachers kill themselves serving a lazy church that won't help them. And he said the Lord will judge that church. That was Finney's belief.

But don't worry about my health. I put my health on the line a long time ago. The Lord can have my health. Why would I want to hang around a turkey world like this after my work is done? Why vegetate and hang around, the last leaf on the tree in the fall, the last rose of summer withered and wilted and pathetically hanging on the end of the stem, waiting for the first wind?

Give your health to the Lord, and then your life itself. People are so afraid to pour out their lives to the Lord. I know a preacher who was told he had angina pectoris and if he didn't take care, he'd die. So he whimpered like a puppy that had been spanked and went off to California and retired. But another friend of mine was told the same thing, and he said, "That's all right. I want to die in God's kingdom in God's work." So he kept on working.

One morning his wife got up to make breakfast and went to wake up her husband, and there was my good friend, lying on the floor, a great tall handsome fellow, stone dead. He had given his last breath to his God. He hadn't gone to California and pulled in his horns and said, "I'm afraid I'll die." Die, brother, for God's sake die! It's all right. You can afford to do it. It's the last thing most people ever do and it's not at all bad. Give yourself to God. "O, God, be exalted above my health. Be exalted above my life."

And don't worry about the length of your days. A long time ago, the Lord gave me two verses: "I will give you a full life span" (Exodus 23:26b) and "Your strength will equal your days" (Deuteronomy 33:25b), and I've been living by them.

We worry too much about our health. People in the world don't. A president or vice president of a big concern comes staggering home at 11 at night with a briefcase and says to his wife, "I had an awful day at the office." And his doctor says, "If you don't look out, you'll die. You're in terrible shape." But he goes right on living like that. Why? To make sales so he can have a bigger yacht next year and a bigger car the year after that. He goes right on working for money.

When the doctor tells you, "You need to protect your health," don't take it too seriously. And when some doctor says, "You need to ease up on your work for the Lord," you should answer, "Goodbye, Doc. I knew the Lord before I knew you." Go ahead and you'll live anyhow. I've found that people who

GIVE

stop working and try to protect their health will tumble over and be finished off in no time. Give up your friendships, your possessions, your comforts, your ambitions, your reputation, your health and even your life, and you'll find that God will give it all back to you, "pressed down, shaken together and running over" (Luke 6:38).

This kind of teaching is very hard to comprehend, because it's not the kind we hear now. We hear something else altogether. Breezy, self-confident Christians tell us how wonderful it is to accept Christ and then have a good time all the rest of your life; the Lord won't demand anything of you. Yes, He will, my friend! The Lord will demand everything of you. And when you give it all up to Him, He may bless it and hand it back, but on the other hand He may not. Remember Betty and John Stam (missionaries to China at the time of the communist revolution)? The communists led the Stams out and they said, "Now, you give up this Christ business or you die."

And the Stams said, "We will not give up Christ."

"All right," they said, "Kneel down." They knelt down. "Bend your head over." They bent their heads over. And John and Betty Stam were beheaded.

We have Christians who have been called upon to give all. But they're richer than Midas, richer than all the kings of the earth, richer than all of the misers of the world because they were permitted to give themselves to God.

One of the great saints of God, back in Roman days

when they were killing Christians, had a desire to die as a martyr. And he wrote to his friends, Christians in Rome, saying "I want to ask a favor of you. I have a yearning in my heart to die for my Lord. I've lived for Him and I've given my all, but it is not enough. I want a crown to set on all other crowns; I want to die for my Lord's sake."

And he said, "The way things are going, I'll die; they've got me sentenced. If you intercede, you can get me off. Please, for Christ's sake, don't do it; don't go to the authorities and ask to get me off. You'll disappoint me and do me a disservice. I'm an old man and I've given my all and now I want this crown. Let me have it. Let me alone."

They didn't intercede and the Romans carried out their sentence. And so that man got his crown, thank God. That's the roster of the spiritually great. What made them like they were? They all found the secret. "O God, be exalted above all. Your kingdom come and my kingdom go." And be sure of one thing, before His kingdom can come, yours has to go. I don't know if that's good eschatology or not. But I know it's good Christian experience, that before the kingdom of Christ can come within me, my kingdom has to go out of me. I have to get off that throne and hand it back to the one to whom it has belonged all these centuries—Jesus Christ our Lord.

Other titles by A.W. Tozer available through your local
Christian bookstore or by calling 1-800-233-4443:

*The Best of A.W. Tozer*
*Born after Midnight*
*The Christian Book of Mystical Verse*
*Christ the Eternal Son*
*The Counselor*
*Echoes from Eden*
*Faith Beyond Reason*
*Gems from Tozer*
*God Tells the Man Who Cares*
*How to be Filled with the Holy Spirit*
*I Call It Heresy!*
*I Talk Back to the Devil*
*Jesus, Author of Our Faith*
*Jesus Is Victor*
*Jesus, Our Man in Glory*
*Let My People Go,* A biography of Robert A. Jaffray
*Man: The Dwelling Place of God*
*Men Who Met God*
*The Next Chapter after the Last*
*Of God and Men*
*Paths to Power*
*The Price of Neglect*
*The Pursuit of God*
*The Quotable Tozer*
*Renewed Day by Day,* Vol. 1
*Renewed Day by Day,* Vol. 2
*The Root of the Righteous*
*Rut, Rot or Revival*
*The Set of the Sail*
*The Size of the Soul*
*That Incredible Christian*
*This World: Playground or Battleground*
*Tragedy in the Church*
*A Treasury of A.W. Tozer*
*The Warfare of the Spirit*
*We Travel an Appointed Way*
*Whatever Happened to Worship*
*When He Is Come*
*Who Put Jesus on the Cross?*
*Wingspread,* A biography of A.B. Simpson